FATHOM Me

*Precious!!
Thank You
For Support
Nirvana Pride*

[signature]
04/17/15

Fathom Me

Nirvana Pride

Copyright © 2014 by Nirvana Pride.

Library of Congress Control Number: 2014913813
ISBN: Hardcover   978-1-4990-5778-2
              Softcover   978-1-4990-5777-5
              eBook   978-1-4990-5779-9

All rights reserved. No part of this book may be reproduced or transmitted in any form or by any means, electronic or mechanical, including photocopying, recording, or by any information storage and retrieval system, without permission in writing from the copyright owner.

Any people depicted in stock imagery provided by Thinkstock are models, and such images are being used for illustrative purposes only.
Certain stock imagery © Thinkstock.

This book was printed in the United States of America.

Rev. date: 09/25/2014

To order additional copies of this book, contact:
Xlibris LLC
1-888-795-4274
www.Xlibris.com
Orders@Xlibris.com
551568

CONTENTS

Prelude 9

Chapter 1	Killing Me Softly	13
Chapter 2	Panic House	15
Chapter 3	Bang, Bang	17
Chapter 4	The Cold Room	20
Chapter 5	Crime Scene	22
Chapter 6	240 Hours	23
Chapter 7	Fathom Not	24
Chapter 8	Eulogy	26
Chapter 9	Devil in the Red Dress	28
Chapter 10	Slow Esteem	29
Chapter 11	Blackarella	33
Chapter 12	Knock, Knock	35
Chapter 13	Time to Bounce	37
Chapter 14	Liberated Missy	41
Chapter 15	Hooky	42
Chapter 16	The Bailout	44
Chapter 17	The Heist	46
Chapter 18	Almost Established	49
Chapter 19	Just Living	51
Chapter 20	Getting Out	53
Chapter 21	The Call	56
Chapter 22	JOB (Jumping on the Boulevard)	58
Chapter 23	The Dance	61
Chapter 24	Addiction	65
Chapter 25	Chicago	66
Chapter 26	The Drive	69
Chapter 27	The Wait	71
Chapter 28	Party Yacht	73

Chapter 29	Approached Rapidly	75
Chapter 30	Home Sweet Home	78
Chapter 31	Back to Work	80
Chapter 32	Date Night	83
Chapter 33	The Argument	85
Chapter 34	Preparation	87
Chapter 35	The Baby Celebration	89
Chapter 36	Delivery	91
Chapter 37	Welcome Back	93
Chapter 38	Intimihaters	96
Chapter 39	Shattered Love	98
Chapter 40	Vulnerable by Fault	100
Chapter 41	Mailed Proposal	102
Chapter 42	Wedding Plans	104
Chapter 43	The Invitation	105
Chapter 44	Probed	107
Chapter 45	Honesty First	109
Chapter 46	Everything Seems Perfect	110
Chapter 47	The Night Before	111
Chapter 48	Not Reality	112
Chapter 49	The Wedding Channel	114
Chapter 50	One Month Later . . . On the Bay in Coronado	117
Chapter 51	When Reality Became Reality	119
Chapter 52	Fourth Time Around	121
Chapter 53	Push	123
Chapter 54	Early A.M.	124
Chapter 55	Baby, These Are My Confessions	125
Chapter 56	Confrontation	127
Chapter 57	Karma Jolt	129
Chapter 58	I Hope You Read My Letter	131
Chapter 59	Expired Visit	133
Chapter 60	Incomplete	134

About the Author	142
About NVme Boutique	144
Extras	146
Index	147

Dedications

This book is dedicated to many people who have come into my life and blessed me with the opportunity to put all my experiences into fathomable words.

First, I would like to dedicate this book to my husband, who has always been there for me through good and bad times. I would like to say thank you for supporting me on everything I dreamed of and helping me make it a reality.

Next, I would like to thank my four wonderful boys—Antonio, Rayshawn, Tahaje, and Jallele—for giving me the opportunity to be their mother, parent, and friend. You are all my creations of *art*. It was time for a change, and I needed to set an example for all of you. My main goal is to make all of you have an extraordinary life. You all mean everything to me, and I love you deeply.

I would also like to thank all my family and friends who have supported me on all my endeavors and believed in me. I would personally like to thank Aesha Akbar, my stylist and friend for life. Not only did you encourage me, you helped me make this a reality. Tonya Blackmon, my counselor. Dione Genaovargas (Remember when we used to sit up and say we were going to write a book and tell the world how we're really feeling? Well, it's a work in process, and I am doing it) and Latesha McCaffety (I love you, girl. I told you I was gonna do this.). I also want to thank my cousin Michele Robinson-Terry and her lovely mother, my aunt Sweetie. I love you both dearly. I never thought in a million years that I would be dedicating this book to my mother-in-law. There isn't really any need for me to elaborate on why this book is dedicated to you. After you read this *amazing* story, I am sure you will then be able to fathom my reasons. This book is not meant to put anyone on a pedestal or to look down on anyone but just to acknowledge the fact that if it had not been for you, I would not have been able to do any of this. They say what doesn't kill you only makes you stronger. I must agree that is absolutely true. So I say to all of you, thank you.

Prelude

I want to take the time to introduce myself. Some may not know me, but you will after you read my amazing story, *Fathom Me*. This is my therapeutic transcript. This was inspired by a journey that was walked by me for several years. Along my journey, there was hurt that men had caused in my life. I had a choice not to accept it, but I did. As women, we all deserve to be treated with respect and integrity.

I have had people ask me, if I had to describe myself as something, what it would be? I thought about it for a moment because that was not a question I wanted to answer right away even though I had tons of answers. After careful consideration of something positive and over-the-top, I came up with water. Nothing is something without water. Water is the liquid that penetrates waterless materials and turns them into a finished product. Water hydrates our thirsty souls and quenches our thirst. Water can tame fires and help you rejuvenate. Water is calm, but water also has wrath. I believe that I am all these things. When you are someone's water supply, that person cannot obtain without you.

The purpose of this book is to let people know that no matter what your struggles are, you can overcome them by faith and willpower, especially when you listen to that little voice of wisdom telling you that what you are about to do is going to not only inspire others but make them admire you for your courage.

It's our destiny to be happy before we leave this earth. I am a Christian, and I know that there is a higher power. I am not perfect, and I do not pretend to be. You get what you see. I am a package deal.

There are so many things that I should have confronted people with, but instead, I let them go, not realizing how they would one day hold me back. The time in my life came to where I had to put myself first.

As a woman, you have to take care of yourself. There is no way possible that you can keep up with the high demand of reality if you are not stress-free. I speak of stress because a lot of women are living in refuge. I imprisoned myself for such a long time. In order to get to where I am now, I had to obtain my main goal, which was to feel *amazing*. The imprisonment had to end.

Letting Go

Forgiveness plays a major role in everyone's life. You can't move on in life holding grudges against people, thinking you are going to come out on top. So many times, I had deep-seated feelings of resentment. No one ever knew how I was feeling. I was very vengeful at times. One day, I had an epiphany about what my purpose was and what I wanted to really do in life. I realized that I would have to start by forgiving all the people who had hurt me. Although it was painful and some folks had not yet experienced my wrath, I knew it was time.

I used to hold grudges against anyone who had done me wrong. The crazy thing is that they wouldn't even know that I was waiting patiently to poison them with my venom. As I started to explore my spiritual side, I had then realized that in order for me to achieve my goals in life and to feel *amazing* about what I was going to accomplish, I would have to forgive everyone. I knew I could never forget, but letting go was something I had to do. Ever since I have thrown out the deep, resentful feelings I once hauled around on this long journey, I have seen tremendous changes in my life. I still get hurt, but that is life. Life is not meant to be picture-perfect. That was something I just had to accept.

Evident Truth

My grandmother—my father's mother—raised me and took me in when I was eight years old, after my mother was murdered in Fayetteville, North Carolina. She had taken custody of my older two brothers as well. Back then, it was like a tug-o'-war because every family member was trying to adopt us for obvious reasons. Of course, my grandmother won the custody battle, since she was the closest living relative to us.

When my grandmother welcomed us into her home, it was OK for about two weeks. Slowly and suddenly, she began to change. I never knew why this lady hated me so much. She kept food on the table. I was never hungry. This hatred was much more than mistreating or neglecting a child of their physical needs. It was more like a rage of jealousy.

My grandmother would buy me clothes that I could not wear. My clothes would just sit in my drawers for months, even years. By the time I was able to wear them, they had either gotten too small or one of my cousins had taken it upon themselves to wear my clothes. Every time I went to school, my friends that lived in my neighborhood with me would always ask me why I could never wear any of my new clothes. They always noticed that my cousins, whom I resided with, could wear theirs. Most of the time, I would have on the same clothes for weeks because I feared what would happen to me if I wore them and was told not to. As soon as my aunts—my mother's sisters—would come and take me out for a day on the town with them, that would be the only time that my grandmother would let me wear my new clothes. It was like she was trying to fool them into thinking everything was all good. I used to tell my aunts what was going on, but when they confronted my grandmother, I was always the liar or the girl who cried wolf.

After growing up and being able to take care of my own needs, my self-esteem had been stomped all over like it had been in a train wreck and like someone had found my self-esteem in the debris of a crashed plane.

Fully Unsuited

In order for me to prepare myself for the future I wanted, I had to stand in front of a mirror and slowly undress myself. After I fully undressed, I started to cry. All my life, I had been told that I was ugly and that I wasn't going to amount to much. I had to realize that the life I had been given is what my Creator has given me. At this time in my life, I did not know how to be thankful for what I had already had. Even though I had not realized that I was already blessed, it was time to make something out of what my Creator had already blessed me with. I didn't have a bachelor's or master's degree gracing my shoulders, but I knew about money and how to get it.

After I looked at myself in the nude, I asked myself these questions.

What was wrong with me? I took out a pad of paper and a pen and wrote down my flaws. I knew that one of my flaws was not believing in myself, having slow self-esteem because of what I let a person say or do to me. I say slow because my self-esteem at this point was not just low—it was going to take time to rebuild that confidence that I never knew I could obtain.

The next question was, what was going to make me happy? I wrote down my desires, which were to have a man that respects me, my mind, body, and time. I wanted and needed to have a man who was able to fathom that if I could make major life-changing alterations to my life for them, then they should be able to do the same for me. I also wanted to obtain my own business. The plan has always been a clothing store because I was a shopaholic and I just loved fashion. Last was to create wealth for generations to come.

The next question was, how was I going to make this happen? I paused before I wrote anything else because I knew what I wanted was far from my reach. All my plans seemed far-fetched. I didn't have all the money in the world, and I didn't even have a starting point. I had nothing. So I stood there, looking at myself until I came up with an answer.

Hours later, I had an answer. It was like a voice had spoken to me and told to make it happen. The voice told me that anything and everything is possible, that I just needed to believe and step out on faith.

The next day, I woke up, and I was then able to dress myself appropriately for what I planned to pursue, because I had peeled back all the malignant layers of what was holding me back. I have always wanted my own business. I have always wanted to maintain my beauty and my great looks, and I have always wanted a man who respected me and my feelings. No doubt about that. What more can you really ask for? If you could have all those in that order, why does anything else matter? I really hope I can captivate your attention so that you will keep reading. This story is based on true life events of my long journey and on other individuals whom I have encountered along my journey. Names and locations have been changed for the privacy of others.

Chapter 1

Killing Me Softly

It was a warm sunny day. Nirvana and her mom, Bobbie, had just arrived in Fayetteville, North Carolina. It had been a long bus ride, and Nirvana was glad it was over. It had taken them almost three days to arrive. You would have thought that Nirvana and her mom would be used to the ride since they had traveled down South a billion times.

Nirvana's mom would always leave Nirvana's two older brothers back home in Saint Louis with family while she traveled. Nirvana was her baby girl. Bobbie needed Nirvana by her side at all times. Nirvana was her only girl and was spoiled rotten.

Bobbie was really anxious to see her sister, Sergeant Maxine Collins, who was serving in the army and had just returned home from across seas fighting a war. They waited patiently for Maxine to pick them up from the Greyhound Bus station. When Maxine arrived, she gave them both heartfelt hugs and took them out for dinner. While Maxine and Bobbie reminisced on old times while waiting for the waiter to bring out what they had ordered, Nirvana combed her Barbie doll's hair, fancying the doll's hair up with bright colored barrettes.

Later, Bobbie and Maxine were to go meet up with their younger sister, Empress. Empress was fair-skinned, thin, had a long, curly mane, and was loudmouthed. Empress was always fighting, light-fingering someone, or worse. Both Bobbie and Maxine loved their sister, but Bobbie's skin crawled just being around her. They were all close, but they both knew Empress wasn't about good deeds.

Bobbie and Nirvana resided in a trailer park with Maxine, while Empress lived on the other side of town, in the suburbs where it went down. This was where the thugs, drunks, and drug peddlers all hung out, and Empress yearned just for that.

Chapter 2

Panic House

It was a few days before Labor Day. Bobbie decided to go over Empress's house down in the suburbs because Maxine had been called to duty and was not due back home for at least thirty-six hours. Bobbie was afraid of being alone since Nirvana's father was all she had ever known. Even though she didn't like Empress's lifestyle, she decided to stay the weekend at her house.

The neighborhood was nice to Nirvana. She was only eight, so it's not like it mattered anyway. Nirvana had met friends who had bikes and swings. Maxine didn't have any of that stuff. She was always gone and had no kids. Empress's street had about seven houses on it. There were four homes on the left side of the street and three on the opposite side. Empress's house was on the side with the three houses. Toward the far end of the street, there was a dead end with an entrance leading into the woods, which had a walkway that led to an elementary school.

Empress's house looked weird to Nirvana. It was bright yellow, with a swing that hung from a tree in the front yard. To the right of Empress's house was an empty lot about half the size of a football field before being able to see the next house on Empress's side of the street. Inside was a small living room with an old sofa against the wall, one window right above the couch, and a television straight ahead in the corner. To the left was the kitchen that had a chained-up gate that had a huge padlock on it. Empress had told Bobbie it was locked and it kept the bad guys out and that she had no key to it. To the right of the kitchen was a bedroom that Empress told Bobbie she could sleep in, since she was planning to be out that night.

Nirvana decided to go back in the living room to watch cartoons. She heard Empress open a door to something she assumed was the closet and tell Bobbie in a whispering voice, "Hey, this is where I keep all the towels, soap, and whatever you need. These are my shoes way up top here, but you see that purple box? Don't touch it. That's where I keep my gun. The only person that knows it's here is me, you, and Rick. And his ass is in jail. He had been threatening me, telling me he was gone kill me. He was supposed to be getting out this weekend. I hope his ass doesn't."

Bobbie had a look of concern on her face because she knew what Empress had done to Rick. Bobbie had been to North Carolina several other times without Nirvana, and every time she would return, she would call their other sister Louise and gossip to her about how Empress's boyfriend had gotten locked up and left her with at least a key of that white girl, a gun, his Caddy, and ten grand. Empress's boyfriend had told her to put it all up in a safe place until he was released or he would kill her. The Caddy she could drive. Of course, with Empress being the person she was, she spent all his money, sold his car, and as far as the drugs, they were never recovered.

Later that night, Bobbie gave Nirvana a bath, rubbed her down with shea butter, and they both cuddled up on the couch together and watched television. As they started to doze off at about 1:00 a.m., they heard a noise, like someone was trying to pry open the window. Bobbie jumped up and ran in the room and told Empress, "Someone is trying to get in through the window!" Bobbie was very shaken up.

Empress came out and looked but didn't see anyone. She laughed in a sleepy, snickering voice and said, "It's probably just Rick. He knows he ain't getting in here. Y'all go back to sleep."

Chapter 3

Bang, Bang

Labor Day had finally arrived. Nirvana was supposed to start school the following day, Tuesday.

When she went outside, she could smell the barbecue grills going. Families were out enjoying what was supposed to be a perfect day.

Marco, Nirvana's friend she had met while she was there, let her ride his bike. She was having the time of her life. Nirvana rode up and down the dead-end street as fast as she could. As she came back down the street, she saw her mom giving her the signal to stop. After Nirvana approached her mother, she was given a sock full of change and was told to go to the store a block or two up the street and buy whatever she wanted. Nirvana gave her mom a kiss on the cheek and snatched the sock full of change and sped off up the street.

Nirvana's day was only getting better, she thought. She rode Marco's bike up the street to Mr. Sam's Packaged Liquor while her mom waited on the corner until she returned. Nirvana got what she wanted and rode the bike back in full speed toward her mom.

She stopped Nirvana again and said to her, "I don't have any money if Empress asks you. I told her I was broke. I hid my money so she wouldn't take it. So go ahead and play now. Just remember, OK?"

Nirvana nodded, letting her mom know she understood. Nirvana was her mom's best friend. Even though she was young, she always followed her instructions and always kept her secrets.

Nirvana rode the bike back up the street to Marco's house to share the goodies she had gotten from the store.

Nirvana and her friends were sitting on the porch, getting sugared up and planning out their next activity. Marco wanted to go catch worms and decapitate them, while his sister wanted to blow up water balloons and bomb folks. All Nirvana wanted to do was ride Marco's bike, since she didn't have one of her own.

She told them she would pass those—she could chop worms up anytime and make water bombs another time. Nirvana then got up and jumped on Marco's bike, and she began to ride up and down the street as fast as she could, popping small wheelies that her brothers had taught her to do.

As she made another round up the street toward the dead end, she came flying back down in full speed. She could see her mother running off the porch steps of Empress's house toward her. Even though she was riding Marco's bike in full speed, it seemed like her mother was running to her in slow motion. As she got closer to her mother, she could see two quarter-size red stains on her shirt. One stain was on her chest, near her heart, and the other stain was diagonally under the first stain.

Bobbie looked at Nirvana, spooked and gasping for breath, and said, "Baby, help me, help me. I have been shot. Somebody has shot me."

At first, Nirvana responded by saying, "Mommy, stop playing."

Then her mother fell to the ground. She could hear the impact of her mother's body hitting the ground. Nirvana dropped the bike and ran to her.

Bobbie told Nirvana to go get help. "Someone has shot me," she continued to say in a faint voice.

Nirvana immediately ran over to Marco's house, busted through the front door, and screamed to Marco's mom, who was on the phone laughing it up and drinking a glass of wine. She said, "Help! My mom is hurt. She said someone shot her."

Marco's mother started to scream loudly, saying, "No, no, no, baby, no!" She hung up the phone and called for help.

When Nirvana went back outside, she tried to get close to her mom, who was lying on the ground reaching out for her. Nirvana tried to go to her, but there was a large crowd of peddlers, drunks, and no-lives standing around her and looking at her while drinking and holding forty-ounce beer bottles in brown paper bags.

Bobbie kept reaching out for Nirvana, but Nirvana was scared to go near her with all those folks standing around her. A family that lived two houses up the street ran down to her with blankets to prop her head on to comfort her. Nirvana's mom was dying in front of her eyes. She kept reaching for Nirvana to come by her side. Nirvana stood there, scared, not knowing how to react.

Soon the ambulance arrived. They pulled out the stretcher, and the other paramedics surrounded her, cutting off all her clothes to see where the bullets had wounded her. She was completely naked in the middle of the street, with all those vermin standing around her like she was some freak show. Before they cut her clothes from her body, she had had on some jeans that were unbuttoned and unzipped, a cropped sweatshirt with no bra, and some black flip-flops. After the paramedics cut her clothes from her body, they then lifted her up on the stretcher and put her into the ambulance.

"Hey, this is her baby girl!" someone yelled from the crowd.

A paramedic then turned around to grab Nirvana and put her on the ambulance with them for a short time while they performed whatever they had to do to save her mother's life.

Shortly, her aunt Maxine arrived at the scene. Marco's mom had called her at work to tell her something bad had happened. Maxine approached the ambulance and stepped on.

Nirvana was sitting on the side of all the chaos, where one of the paramedics had placed her. Suddenly, Bobbie lifted her head up and reached out for both Nirvana and Maxine and tried to tell them something. The words uttered off her tongue saying in a faint voice, "Som-som-sombod-somebody . . ."

While Bobbie tried to utter her last words, the paramedics shoved her head back down onto the stretcher. Her eyes rolled back in her head, and her body shivered violently as she exhaled her last breath of oxygen.

Nirvana had just seen her mother die right before her eyes.

Maxine screamed, "Why did you do that? No! Why did you do that? She was trying to tell me something! No! Why?"

Someone then opened the back door to the ambulance and pulled Aunt Maxine from the ambulance. They told her to take Nirvana with her and meet them at the Fayetteville Hospital. Aunt Maxine then put Nirvana in the car, without a seat belt, and rushed to the hospital in full speed, silently crying with bloodshot eyes.

Chapter 4

The Cold Room

When they arrived at the hospital, Maxine was greeted by the head nurse, who must have known why they were there. Marco's mom had followed Maxine and Nirvana to the hospital for support.

"Please follow me," the nurse said. She opened up a door to a room that had three small conjoining benches connected against the walls and one window that looked like it had barbed wire on the outside of it and offered them a seat. The room was cold and nippy.

Nirvana was still in shock. She knew what had happened, but she had not digested it all. Everything was still sitting in the roof of her mouth. She felt sick to her stomach. The room they were in smelled of disinfectant, vomit, and what she thought death smelled like, she thought to herself while waiting. She knew something was wrong. She could feel it. The room was cold, and Maxine was pacing the floor back and forth. Marco's mom was sitting on the bench, shaking her legs and rocking back in forth.

Suddenly the door opened. Maxine looked up, hoping it was the doctor with good news; instead, it was Empress. Maxine said to her, crying and sobbing, "Bobbie was shot."

Empress replied and said, "I know. I saw it on the news. Did y'all know it was on the news?" Empress looked very cold, like what had happened didn't faze her. She was calm and collected while everyone else was on edge. She had a sneaky smirk about her face. She was dressed in an all-black hoodie, dark denim jeans, and black classic Reebok tennis shoes.

The door then opened slowly, and the doctor came in to rip the bad news. "Mrs. Collins, I'm so sorry. We did all we could. She didn't make it. She was shot twice in the heart, up close. With both wounds being less than an inch from her heart and an inch of each other, they caused her to bleed internally and drown in her own fluids," he said as he held his head down, as if this was the worst part of his job.

Maxine screamed and screamed, "*No! No! No!* This can't be! She has kids."

Empress sat back with no expression at all. She was calm and spacey. She just sat there while everyone else was grieving.

Chapter 5

Crime Scene

Empress's house was now a crime scene. Maxine drove back to the scene with detectives to see if they could add up what happened. Everything was a blur to Maxine, and she was trying to fight one of the worst headaches she had ever experienced in her life.

Empress told Maxine that the detectives had already questioned her and fingerprinted her before she came to the hospital and that they were trying to say that Nirvana's mom had killed herself because her fingerprints were the only prints found in Empress's house.

When Maxine had spoken with the detectives, they shared with her that her sister's bloody fingerprints were all over the house. They also told her what was weird was that they couldn't find a trace of Empress's prints when it was her house in the first place. Maxine then asked the detectives if they had started to fingerprint and test anyone near the scene for gunpowder residue. They informed her they had not started to do anything because they were trying to rule out foul play.

Maxine was very confused but knew whatever Empress was telling her was not the whole truth. She didn't understand why Empress would tell her that she had been fingerprinted. Although Maxine didn't want to think about it, she felt deep inside that Empress played a part in whatever happened in her house and was trying to cover it up. Maxine started to think very hard. Maxine could remember all the stories Bobbie had told her about Empress. As thoughts chased through Maxine's mind, she realized that she didn't recall Empress having any ink on her hands while she claimed that she had been fingerprinted.

Chapter 6

240 Hours

It had been a long ride back to Saint Louis. Maxine had her sister's body transported back to Saint Louis, where all her family resided. The funeral was to be in twelve days at Jackson & Jackson Funeral Home.

Nirvana had not eaten in days. Maxine had tried to feed her Jell-O and broth, but she didn't budge.

When they arrived in Saint Louis, the family had gotten together to make funeral arrangements and to see who was going to take custody of Nirvana and her two older brothers. Nirvana's grandmother, who was her father's mother, petitioned the courts for custody and won.

Nirvana still was trying to get over everything she had seen over the past week. She couldn't believe that her best friend was gone. Later that week, Maxine and Louise took Nirvana to find a dress to wear to the funeral. What they had gotten her was a cheap dusty-pink dress from the church shop in the city, on Cass Avenue.

Nirvana's grandmother Kat sent for her to go get her hair fixed up by their second oldest cousin Cupcake. After all the plans were finalized, the days drifted away as it was time to celebrate the existence of Nirvana's mom.

Chapter 7

Fathom Not

It was hard for Nirvana to understand what was going on in her life at the time. All she knew was that her best friend was gone. Last time she recalled her mom had just taken her to go ride the ponies at a local farm in Fayetteville, North Carolina. It was the best time of her life.

Now she was trapped in a home of envious people who only wanted her for what was left behind. They never had any good intentions. Although Nirvana had two older brothers, it seemed as if they were never around. She was lonely. She was looking for answers. She was already devastated that she had never known her father because he was killed when she was only four months old—on Independence Day, trying to protect his loudmouthed brother who seemed to keep up more trouble than the KKK.

Nirvana always asked questions about her father, but they always went unanswered. She would always ask, "Mom, where is Dad? Why is he never around? Did something bad happen to him?"

Her mom would always break down into a fistful of tears and say, "Your dad was a wonderful man. He was a damn good man, but he died, baby, when you were only four months old. Your brothers were a few years older, and they remember him, but I know there is no way you ever could." Bobbie started to tell Nirvana how it happened. Nirvana sat there and listened carefully. At the time, she was only six years old, but she wanted to know.

"OK, baby," Bobbie said to her baby girl. "It was on a nice, sunny Fourth of July day. I and the family had barbecued. It was tons of us having a good time. Next thing you know, Wex, your dad's cousin, came running through the side gate of the house leading to the backyard where me and your dad, your uncles and cousins, and other family members were partying so hard. I was drinking a beer and holding you in my arms while playing cards all at the same time when Wex yelled desperately, 'They're gonna kill 'im! They're gonna kill 'im! They got 'im! They got Billy. He called Shot Gun's wife a bitch! Now they're beating him up.'

"Your dad suddenly jumped up from the card table and took off, jumping the fence that led to the alley where they had Billy. Before you know it, we all heard two shots fired. Boom! Boom! Another sounded off moments later. I gave you to your grandmother—your dad's mother—and took off toward the alley, and I saw your father lying in a puddle of his own blood. His body was lifeless. It was like he had died instantly. I went up to him and held him in my arms screaming, 'What have you done? What have you done?' Shot Gun took off, running down the alley along with his brothers and wife. I kissed your father's lifeless body and laid his head down on the ground gently. I got up and started to chase Shot Gun until he vanished out of my sight."

She told Nirvana while holding her in her arms. "When we all arrived at the hospital, the coroner told us he was shot twice. Once in the neck and once in the jaw, and a bullet traveled down and punctured his heart and lungs, which caused him to drown in his own fluids."

Chapter 8

Eulogy

It had been Nirvana's first time riding in a limousine. You would think her first ride in a luxury vehicle would be because she was finally famous. There were two long black stretch limos that transported both sides of the family to Jackson and Jackson Funeral Home. Behind them was a bulky large black car that Nirvana had no idea that her mother's lifeless body was in.

As the funeral began, you could hear Kat, Nirvana's grandmother, screaming and yelling before the funeral had started. Kat was such a drama queen. She wore a long black dress with knee-length slits on the side, with plain black shoes with about a two-inch rise, and a large veiled hat that hid her face almost completely.

As the funeral began, the choir sang two selections, and then the eulogy was done by Rosie, a really close friend of Nirvana's mother. Nirvana had only gotten to know her mother for eight years. She didn't really know much about her. To Nirvana, her mother was a normal person. The evening of the funeral, she heard everyone say nothing but good things about her mother—how she was sweet and caring, how most often folks took advantage of her kindness but she always found a way to forgive. Nirvana also found out that her mother was schizophrenic and had multiple personalities but was not considered to be a threat to anyone. Bobbie always smiled and went with the flow. They said she lost it after she saw Nirvana's father killed. That was all her mother had really known. He was her first and her last. She had worked but didn't really need to because he was the man. After Bobbie saw Nirvana's father die, she had a nervous breakdown. Nirvana also found out that her mom was really into fashion. At the funeral, Rosie spoke about how Bobbie and Nirvana's father dreamed of opening a clothing store together and making their own fashions and selling them. After the eulogy, it was time to view the body.

As soon as the casket opened, all you could hear was Kat screaming and yelling, "That's not her! Close it! Close it! My Lawd, close the casket! That ain't her. That ain't her, aw, Lawd, what did they do to her?"

Then you could hear Nirvana's grandfather say, "Oh, Kat, shut up! Do you always got tah exaggerate? Got damnit, Kat!" He was frowning.

Everyone was used to my Kat's funeral shows. It was normal to them, but not to Nirvana, since all this was a first-time experience for her.

Kat stopped screaming and said to him, "Oh, Maasawn, kiss my ass!" Then she started to scream again. Kat was the true definition of a drama queen. Onlookers shook their heads, saying things like "They always got to show out in public. They are so dysfunctional."

Nirvana's grandfather Mason thought he was cool. He wore an old tight suit he probably had since pimps had been pimping. He was so out of date, but of course, to him, he was the one.

Nirvana was the first to actually walk up to the casket and view her mother's lifeless body. She had looked like she had been stuffed with cotton; she was cold, stiff, and lifeless. Nirvana still couldn't grasp the reality of what was going on. She just stood there while everyone passed crying and placing roses in her mother's casket and kissing her forehead. Nirvana felt lost.

Chapter 9

Devil in the Red Dress

Everyone except the kids were dressed in black at the funeral of Nirvana's mom, with the exception of Empress, who showed up to the funeral in a loud bludgeon red dress, white panty hose with red hearts, red pumps, and a red hat that veiled her face. Oh yeah, she was fancy. Too damn fancy for a funeral—not to mention her sister's funeral. Everyone looked at her and could not believe what they were seeing. Empress was sitting on the pew closest to the front of the funeral home, playing peekaboo with her son (who was a few years shy of Nirvana), laughing, chewing, and not paying any attention to what was going on at the funeral. Red flag, just like the whole getup she wore. Everyone started to point fingers and shake their head.

Nirvana didn't understand at the time why you shouldn't wear red to a funeral, until she heard the family saying, "Oh my god, do you see her? That is so rude and disrespectful to her sister. What is wrong with her?" Not to mention she wasn't even mourning her sister now. It was like she was in another world. Empress was a ghost. She was so disrespectful.

Weeks after the funeral, Nirvana started to hear rumors of family believing Empress was involved in her mom's death. Nirvana didn't believe it at the time, but as she got older, things started to make more sense and add up. She knew her mom was not a killer. Her mother couldn't even kill a fly, so why kill herself? She questioned herself. And who would and could shoot themselves twice in the chest?

Even though Nirvana was young, all types of scenarios overpoured her thoughts. The Devil in the Red Dress had to have known something. Everyone knew deep inside, but the truth still had not come to light.

Chapter 10

Slow Esteem

"Ohm, you so ugly, *ugly*, uggggggglee!" Nirvana's grandmother said to her early one morning as she went into the kitchen to see if breakfast was ready.

Nirvana was eleven years old when Kat started to say that to her. It was like Kat got a thrill from it. Kat would just laugh while stomping her callused foot on the floor in harmony with her laugh. It took Kat a few times to say those degrading words to Nirvana before Nirvana would cry. As Kat continued to taunt Nirvana, she could see that saying those words to her would eventually make her cry.

The "ugly game" was Kat's family-gathering entertainment. Nirvana would be in her room where she was told she always had to stay unless she was going to school, using the bathroom, or eating a meal. Kat would have family and friends come over and call Nirvana out of her room and say to her houseguest, "Watch this," with a creepy smile that had reminded Nirvana of the Wicked Witch of the East because she had no teeth and her face was partially sunken in. Mason, her husband and Nirvana's grandfather, knocked all her teeth out her mouth because to him, she ran off at the mouth too much.

Kat would have everyone form a circle around Nirvana while she taunted her by calling her ugly in various tones while laughing and having a good ol' time. Kat would say to everyone else, "Watch this. I mahhh make her cry."

Everyone would just sit around with Kat and laugh, until one day, Kat's stepdaughter Kelly made a stand and yelled out loud above everyone, saying, "OK, Kat, that is enough! I will not hang around for this. You do this every single time we get together! That's not fair that this child has to go through this! And you should be ashamed of yourselves. All of you!" Kelly then took her belongings and left.

Kat would be totally out of breath from laughing and would say, "Take your li'l funky-fast ass on back to your room. You make me sick. I can't stand her. Whew! I just can't stand her."

Nirvana would just go to her room and cry. Sometimes, Nirvana would pray and ask God to let her see her mother just one more time. Nirvana knew it was not going to happen, but as long as she felt she would see her mother again, it made her days and nights somewhat easier to deal with.

Kat had three daughters: Crystal, Mauhget, and Jean. Crystal and Mauhget lived with Nirvana and Kat, and they would also come around and tease Nirvana as well. Jean had gotten married to an Evangelist and was hardly ever around anymore. Crystal and Mauhget had it out for Nirvana day and night. Jean had her moments, but Jean would be the one who would try to defend Nirvana. Every time Jean would defend Nirvana, it made Kat extremely upset. Kat would always scream at Jean, saying, "Why don't you take her home with you with her funky-fast ass?"

Jean would reply, "I will when you are ready to give up her social security check. That is the only reason you adopted them, Mother!" After each time Jean screamed what her heart was feeling, she would always leave abruptly.

When Nirvana's grandmother first adopted her, Vicki, Mauhget's daughter, and Nirvana would always have to take baths together to save water. At the time, Vicki and Nirvana were about ten years old.

One day, Vicki decided to take a piss in the bathwater like a normal kid would do, so Nirvana jumped out of the tub. Vicki looked at Nirvana and said, "Why you getting out? Get back in before I tell my mommah!"

Nirvana looked at her with a yuck face and said, "No!"

Vicki then started to yell as if someone was trying to kill her. "Maaaamahhh! Maaaamahhh!"

Mauhget rushed to the bathroom as if Vicki was dying. "What's wrong, baby?" Mauhget asked.

"Nirvana won't get back in the tub," Vicki said.

Nirvana replied, "Because she peed in the water. Look at it! It's all yellow."

Mauhget looked at Nirvana with a childish grin and pushed her back into the tub then took a face rag and drenched it in the pissy water and started to wash Nirvana's face with it. Dunking the rag back and forth in the water several times, repeating the cycle, singing a tune you can tell she was making up along the way, saying, "Piss is good for you. Hooray! Piss is good for your face. Hooray! Piss—it makes your skin shine. Hooray! Piss—it makes your hair grow. Hooray!" Vicki sat back and giggled.

After their baths were over, Nirvana still felt dirty. She even thought she smelled the urine scent on her hours after they had taken a bath together. For the rest of the day, Vicki continued to tease Nirvana and call her the Piss Washer and tell her she smelled.

Mauhget did anything for Vicki. Vicki was the only child she was actually able to give birth to after about eight miscarriages. They called Vicki the Miracle Child. Vicki always got her way. Even when Nirvana and Vicki brushed their teeth, Mauhget would give Vicki a whole strip of toothpaste on her brush while only giving Nirvana a small dab in the middle of her toothbrush. Nirvana never understood why she was treated like an outcast and had no idea that what she was about to experience was only the beginning.

Federal Grievance

It was hot and muggy outside. Saint Louis humidity was very uncomfortable. Nirvana finally knew the truth about what happened to her father. It still didn't make sense to her why her mother and father had both been taken from her at such an early age. Both of her parents had been killed by violence and both on federal holidays. Her father on Independence Day then her mother on Labor Day. Something was wrong with that picture.

That has to mean something, she thought to herself.

At the time her mother was murdered, it was all a blur. It was surreal, like a bad dream she couldn't wake from. She was sitting on the back porch of her new family's home, recalling all the events that led to her predicament. She had not eaten for days; there was a constant feeling of nausea. Her head was pounding, as if someone was inside it trying to get out. Redbirds were chirping, and children were playing, but Nirvana just moped around. She went into the house—into the biggest and darkest room of the house—and screamed into a pillow until she fell asleep.

Chapter 11

Blackarella

It was seven years and some months later.

"Where's that funky-fast ass winch at?" Kat said to her daughter Mauhget. "Tell her to get up and come scrub these floors 'fore I beat her black ass."

Nirvana heard the steps squeaking as Mauhget's footsteps were approaching her room, which was on the third floor of the house Kat had purchased with all the insurance money she had received from the death of Nirvana's mother. Little did Mauhget know that Nirvana was already up and ready to go, for she had been used to the drill of being pulled out of bed every morning at 5:00 a.m. to do the same chores she had repeatedly done day in and day out for years.

As Mauhget opened the door to Nirvana's room, Nirvana was already up and ready to go. She surprised Mauhget and said, "Yeah, yeah, I already know. You thought you were going to have the pleasure of pulling me out of the bed this time, huh?" Nirvana walked past Mauhget and quickly went downstairs.

As soon as she entered the kitchen, she was smacked dead in the face with a newspaper by Kat. "Go clean those mirrors and windows!" Kat yelled at her. "You were supposed to have cleaned them last night! You make me so, so, so sick, you li'l black child. I can't stand your li'l black funky-fast ass!" Kat continued to yell.

Nirvana never knew why she continued to call her funky-fast, for she wasn't even able to get near any boys—or girls for that matter, if she had been lesbian. Not only that. *What in the hell did* funky-fast *mean?*

Nirvana would always ask herself. Nirvana shed a few tears, picked the newspaper she had been smacked in the face with off the ground, and started to clean the glass mirrors in the dining room as instructed.

"You missed a spot," Mauhget said as she stood over her. "Oh, it's another one right there too." She was laughing and coughing sputum specks on the back of Nirvana's bare neck, which was turned to her. Mauhget had asthma really bad, to the point where she couldn't keep any food down and where she coughed all the time. The smallest thing would upset her, and there she would go, coughing, vomiting, and still trying to talk at the same time. She always had a strong urine smell to her because she always pissed herself when she coughed.

Nirvana continued to clean the glass as instructed then proceeded to the next chores. It was almost noon, and Nirvana's stomach was growling. She was ready to eat but knew she would not be able to until she had scrubbed the floorboards on her hands and knees in the kitchen and bathroom first. All her cousins had eaten and were playing, running through the house, making more of a mess because they knew she was going to have to clean up their messes.

Nirvana was now a teenager, and seventeen was going to be knocking at her door in a matter of weeks. Nirvana was tired and worn out from the previous days' chores. She had been cleaning all day long. *When was it going to end?* she thought to herself. Nirvana had never gone out with her friends. Nirvana's grandmother didn't even let her experience homecoming or prom. She always told Nirvana she was "too damn funky-fast." Nirvana never even came out of her room unless it was time to eat and, of course, clean behind the trifling-ass folks that she had been living with for years.

Chapter 12

Knock, Knock

Nirvana woke up in a great mood although she knew she had no gifts and no one would even say happy birthday to her. She sat there until she heard someone call her name to come eat or clean. No one ever did, so she sat there waiting, wanting to go peek downstairs, but she was too afraid of what might happen if she did. Suddenly she heard her door open slowly.

It was her brother Vadyme. Vadyme came in and wished her happy birthday. "Sis, I don't know how you sit here and take this mess. Man, I am out. You wanna come?" he asked.

She said no. All Nirvana wanted was to be treated like everyone else. She said sadly to her brother, "It's my birthday, and no one has said it to me. Nor have they gotten me a cake. You know, last year when Vicki's birthday came up, they got her a cake. She had on this pretty denim skirt with paint speckles all over it, the cutest shirt, new jellybean sandals. And all her family and friends were invited to come and celebrate with her."

Nirvana complained to Vadyme. Nirvana continued to say to Vadyme, "You know Mauhget, Jean, and Crystal teased me all day for fun and told me I was ugly and that I looked like a banana with clothes on?" Nirvana was really thin for an average teen. Nirvana was straight up and down, with no breast and large nipples that looked like doorbell buzzers. "Yeah, brother, I want to go, but where will I go? I have no one."

Vadyme interrupted her and said, "Man! Look, sis, fuck 'em! You can do this shit on your own. You seventeen now. You don't need them.

I mean, for years, you haven't been able to play with your friends because you were always cleaning. They keep you in this room and only call you out to make fun of you. You missed your homecoming and school dances because Grandma didn't want to get you anything to wear, and she is getting money for all of us. That's fucked up, man! Well, I am about to bounce. You should think about it too." Vadyme gave her a hug and darted down the stairs and out the door.

Nirvana wanted to leave, but she knew no one else. She was also scared of what they might do to her if she tried to leave. Every time she mentioned she wanted to leave, that would be the only time when Kat would say she loved Nirvana. Nirvana knew that what Kat was saying was a lie from the pits of hell. Kat just wanted her for her social-security check. Seventeen years of her life had flown by, and Nirvana had no friends, nor did she know how to act in a public crowd. Nirvana was all the way confused, and it was going to take some time to fix what had been broken for many years.

Chapter 13

Time to Bounce

A few weeks went by, and Nirvana woke up and started to clean the house all by herself without anyone telling her to. Nirvana even went and got the mail out of the mailbox and set it on her grandmother's bed, since she didn't want to put her in a bad mood. All Nirvana's chores were pretty much done, so she decided to go take a chill pill in the room of her oldest cousin, Lil Bitty Bit, and chitchat for a while.

"Lil Bitty Bit, come here!" their grandmother Kat yelled.

Lil Bitty Bit was her cousin's nickname. She had been given that since she was so small and thin but had a huge butt to match. Lil Bitty Bit went to see what their grandmother wanted, and Kat told Lil Bitty Bit to go see if the mailman had run.

Lil Bitty Bit went to look in the mailbox, and there was no mail. "The mail not in there, Grandma. He must didn't run yet," Lil Bitty Bit said to their grandma.

As Lil Bitty Bit headed back toward her room, Nirvana caught her in the hallway and told her, "The mail is on Grandma's bed. I put it there about an hour ago."

Lil Bitty Bit went to get the mail and give it to Kat. Kat looked at her and said, "I thought the mail didn't come?"

"Oh, it did. Nirvana put it on your bed."

Suddenly Kat jumped up and hurried in the room and pushed Nirvana upside the head and said, "Who told you to touch my mail, you li'l winch? Who told you to touch it?"

Nirvana stood up and said, "Well, I didn't want to upset you, so I set it on your bed."

Kat took the cordless telephone she was holding in her hand and hit Nirvana on the head with it. "I can't stand you!" In defense, Nirvana fell to the ground and covered her head while Kat continued to hit her with the phone, saying to her, "You make me sick! You ugly! You always messing with something."

Suddenly Nirvana got off the floor and pushed past her grandmother and ran back into her room, crying.

"You li'l winch! I know you didn't just hit me!" her grandmother yelled, chasing her.

There was a broom in the hallway that her grandmother picked up on the way as she followed Nirvana to her room. Kat started to beat Nirvana with it until it started to break. *Swat! Swat! Swat!* You could hear the broom start to crack as it continued to hit Nirvana across the back.

"Stop it! Stop it! Stop it!" Nirvana yelled. "Why do you hate me so much? What have I done to you? Stop it! I won't take this anymore."

Next thing you know, Kat got the phone she was hitting Nirvana with and called up Mauhget, screaming, "Help me! Help, she just hit me! This li'l winch just hit me!"

Next thing you know, Mauhget called Crystal, then Crystal called Ducc. Ducc was Kat's oldest son who had just retired from US National Coast Guard. For some strange reason, everyone was afraid of him. Don't know why, because Ducc was the biggest pussy.

Within five minutes of being called by his sister Crystal, Ducc arrived at his mother's house because he lived about five minutes away. As Ducc entered the foyer to the entrance of his mother's house, he saw Nirvana standing in the bathroom, washing the tears from her face, and pulled her by her pixie braids. He slapped her three times, acting as if she owed him money for drugs.

Slap! Slap! Slap! Nirvana's face went from side to side. Nirvana yelled, asking him to stop and telling him that everything was not what it seemed.

He stopped and pinned her up against the hallway wall, partially choking her, leaving her with just enough oxygen to breathe small, shallow spurts of air, and asked her, "So you are saying my momma lying on you? My mother doesn't lie! And don't you ever fix your mouth to say she is." Then he let her go, and Nirvana fell to the floor, gasping for air while holding her neck. Ducc then started to take Nirvana's clothes out of the closets and drawers in her room and throw them out on the front lawn, telling her she had to go.

Kat just sat there and watched. Even if Kat wanted to say something in Nirvana's defense, she wouldn't have had the guts to because she was scared of her Ducc.

Moments later, Vadyme pulled up in the driveway in the brand-new Chevy Mustang he had just purchased at an auction. Vadyme had no clue what was going on. Vadyme came in, and Ducc was in the kitchen talking to Kat and Mason like nothing had ever happened.

Nirvana was getting the rest of her belongings so that she could finally leave, because enough was enough.

Vadyme went in Nirvana's room and asked her, "What happened? Why are all your clothes on the front lawn?"

Nirvana replied, "Ducc slapped me because Grandma lied on me and said I hit her when she was the one hurting me."

Vadyme was slow to anger, but when he was upset, there was no stopping him. Vadyme was tired of seeing Nirvana crying and unhappy.

Vadyme went in the kitchen to confront Ducc about his sister when all of a sudden, Nirvana heard a loud, high-pitched metal sound that sounded like something had been hit hard. It was a sound that made her cringe when she heard it. Nirvana rushed out of her room into the kitchen to see what noise could sound so horrible when she saw blood gushing from her brother's head. Vadyme was nicely built and had muscles for days. Vadyme had Ducc in a headlock while blood was gushing out of his head. As she continued to look to see why her brother had so much blood almost pouring from his head, she saw a small cast-iron skillet that her grandmother used to make cornbread griddle cakes on the floor, broken in half with blood all over it.

Kat was sitting at the table, just watching and not saying a thing with her grayish eyes and sunken-in face, looking downward and chewing gum. Mason was preparing bleach water over the sink so that he could hurry and clean up the blood that splattered from the hit and was all over the kitchen floor and on the stove and refrigerator. Ducc was yelling at Vadyme to let him go.

Vadyme yelled, "No! You lucky I can't see right now, or I would kill you." Vadyme continued to keep Ducc in a tight headlock. Even though Vadyme had been hit in the head and blood was in his eyes, he had Ducc in way he couldn't move.

Nirvana jumped over them and ran to the telephone to call the police when Kat suddenly jumped up and snatched the plug from the wall and yelled, "No, you will not call the police. You too fast for your own good."

Nirvana screamed, "This is my brother! Are you crazy? He needs help! He is bleeding everywhere!" So Nirvana ran out the kitchen through the front door, going across the street to Quick Trip to use a pay phone to call for help.

When the ambulance arrived, her grandfather had already cleaned up all the blood. It was so clean you wouldn't have even thought what had happened actually had. When Vadyme decided to let Ducc out of the headlock, Vadyme went out into the yard with a two-by-four stick, about to break all of Ducc's windows in the new BMW he had just purchased.

Nirvana begged Vadyme not to, saying that it wasn't worth it. Nirvana somehow managed to get the stick from Vadyme and calm him down. The police finally arrived to investigate the commotion. Vadyme explained what happened while the paramedics checked him out and told him he needed medical attention and that he should go to the hospital. Vadyme refused. Vadyme was angry and furious. He wanted to fight.

Nirvana ran back in the house to grab some items, leaving all her other belongings on the front lawn. She got into Vadyme's car, and they sped off. Vadyme was furious. Nirvana asked him if he was going to press charges. Vadyme looked at her with a smirk on his face and said, "No, I am going to kill him. He is a dead man."

Chapter 14

Liberated Missy

Nirvana was free. It felt good to be out living on her own. It had been almost two weeks, and she was getting by just fine.

She had been staying wherever she could for the time being, but she was scared. Her friends knew her situation, and they looked out the best they could by sneaking her food down in the basement when their parents were sleeping. Sometimes they would give her money.

Nirvana knew this wouldn't last long. She had to do something. She had no money, no food, and barely any clothes to change into. She felt nervous because she didn't know how to interact with the world, for she had not been fully exposed to it like most of her friends.

Chapter 15

Hooky

Nirvana was sitting in class and needed an excuse to leave. The "I gotta go to bathroom" one didn't work all the time. So she made up something about how she had left her homework in the bathroom. Her instructor, Ms. Russo, excused her and gave five minutes to return to class.

Nirvana had no plans on returning to class because she had a weird feeling in the bottom of her stomach. She knew something was wrong but couldn't figure it out just yet. So she hurried to the bathroom before the janitors locked them up. The janitors were instructed to lock all bathrooms up ten minutes after classes were in session. So she locked herself in a stall in one of the restrooms and stood on the toilet until she heard the doors being locked by the janitors.

It was really weird because she didn't know why she was doing this. She sat there in the stall and relaxed while all kinds of thoughts ran through her head about how she was going to get money and food for the next few days. Next thing you know, there was a knock on the bathroom door. She was scared at first but didn't panic because if it was someone of authority, they could have just unlocked the door.

"Nirvana, are you in there?" she heard a voice whisper. "If you are, girl, open the door. This is Kikka. Open the door."

Nirvana slowly opened the door and let Kikka in. "Hey, what's up?" Nirvana said.

"Girl, it's a good thing you left class."

"Why? What's up?" Nirvana said.

"The police are here. They're looking for you. It's, like, three officers and two detectives."

"For real?" Nirvana said, panicking and trying to understand why they were looking for her.

"Well, I was in the office," Kikka began to tell her. "That's when they walked in, asking the principal questions and showing them a picture of you. All I heard them say is that they were looking for you because your grandmother said you ran away."

"What! Are you serious? You know my loony toon grandmother put—"

"I know, I know," Kikka interrupted. "You don't have to tell me. I already know what's going on and what went down. That's fucked up—her lying on you like that. OK, look, school is almost over with," Kikka said. "I am going to help you sneak out of school, and you can ride the bus home with me. My mom won't mind because I had already been telling her about what's been going on with you anyways for years. So what I am going to do is go back to class like all is normal before they start wondering where I am at, because I left the office like six or seven minutes ago. You already got your stuff, right?"

"Yeah," Nirvana answered.

"OK. Well, I see you in a bit," Kikka replied as she headed for the door.

"Wait! Do you think they gone look in here for me?"

"Girl, hell, naw. They know the janitors lock the doors after class, and not to mention, those lazy-ass janitors don't even check the stalls before they lock up. If they did, you wouldn't be in here. OK, I gotta go. Lock the door back. I will see you in a bit."

Chapter 16

The Bailout

The last bell of the day was about five minutes from ringing. Nirvana waited patiently for Kikka to return to the bathroom. Moments later, Kikka returned to the door and knocked and said, "It's me. Let me in."

Nirvana opened the door, and immediately, they started to plot their escape as if they were really criminals. They made jokes while plotting a good plan.

"Girl, make sure you brush your teeth when you get to my house. Your breath smells like sardines and ass," Kikka said jokingly, but she was also serious.

Nirvana took no offense because she hadn't brushed her teeth in about three days and found the remark funny, saying, "I know, right?"

"OK, we got like three minutes before the bell rings. I told Mrs. Parkinson that I had left something at the office, so she dismissed me early. I went back up to the office to take a peek, and they got an officer standing on each side of the exit doors leading to the buses. And it looked like they were holding a picture of you too," Kikka told Nirvana.

Nirvana had this freakishly oversize black coat with an extra-large puffy hood, gloves, and skullcap. She put all that on, and Kikka gave her a scarf to cover the bottom half of her face.

"OK, my bus number is 2098. It's the third bus down from the last. Just walk out normal like everybody else, and get on my bus. I will be right behind you. Just act normal, and they won't even notice you with all the junk on."

Ring! Ring! Ring! The bell went off. Nirvana and Kikka stayed in the bathroom for about two extra minutes to give the halls a chance to fill up with eager students ready to go home. As the halls flooded with students, they both drifted in the crowd like everybody else.

As Nirvana approached the exit to the school, she could see the officers looking at what seemed to be a photo and every student that passed them. She was getting closer, and her heart was pacing. Her hands were sweating. As she exited the school, she heard one of the officers say, "Excuse me, Nirvana?" Her stomach dropped, but she kept walking and proceeded to bus 2098.

Chapter 17

The Heist

The first of the month was creeping around, and Nirvana needed money badly. Kikka's mother had taken her in like her own child. It had been nearly two weeks since their criminal escape. Nirvana knew her grandmother Kat was receiving social-security benefits for her of $827 a month. She just needed a way to get that money. She was ready to be out on her own.

While Nirvana was thinking up a way to get her check, Kikka walked into the kitchen where Nirvana was eating Cocoa Puffs, and they started immediately thinking of a way to nab that check. Kikka told Nirvana that she had a guy friend with a car and that she could get him to take them over there early that morning and just wait for the mailman. Nirvana agreed, and Kikka arranged everything else.

It was finally the first of the month, and Nirvana couldn't sleep, for she was anxious to get her hand on that check. It was about 8:30 a.m., and she and Kikka were getting ready and waiting for Ronzell, Kikka's friend, to arrive. They had to get there early because the mailman normally ran his route between 10:00 and 11:00 a.m.

At nine o'clock sharp, Ronzell was outside honking his horn for them to come out. They hopped in the car, went to the gas station about two houses down from the house of Nirvana's grandmother, and waited patiently. Within fifteen minutes, they spotted the mailman turning the corner to come onto the lot of the gas station. They thought that it was odd because he was extremely early, but he ran in and got a coffee, and Nirvana was waiting at his mail truck with her state ID when he returned. She said, "Excuse me, Mr. Mailman. I live right there, two houses up at 12234 Lake Harley Road, and I was just trying to see if you had some mail for me. I am expecting a check."

The mailman looked at her suspiciously and took her ID. He compared her name to what was on the check and gave it to her. Nirvana snatched the check and got back in the car, and the group sped off, laughing and giving each other high fives, saying, "Yeah, we did it."

"Now you got to try to cash it," Kikka said.

"I know the check is in my grandmother's name for me. She has to cash it," Nirvana said.

"Man, fuck that! All you got to do is go to the social security office and tell them what's going on, and they will put it in your name. You don't live there anymore. Your grandmother can't expect to keep getting all that money for you, and you're not there!" Kikka exclaimed. "Ronzell, do you have time to take her to the social security office?"

"Yeah, I can do that. I ain't doing nothing all day that I know of."

Ronzell took them to the social security office. Nirvana went in, grabbed a number, and waited to be called. Moments later, she was able to approach a window and talk to a lady that was really nice.

"How may I help you on this lovely day?" the clerk asked.

Nirvana told the lady the situation and showed her the check. She also told the lady that she was not residing with her grandmother anymore and her grandmother was still trying to get her check.

The lady smiled and said, "This is what I am going to do for you. This is your lucky day. First, let me see some identification, and I am going to get this switched over to your name. Now this check here will have to be reissued, and it will take about three to five business days for you to receive a new one.

"Sweetie, we see this all the time. The guardians put their kids out and still expect to get their money. That's just ridiculous!" The lady shook her head. "You have the option to go over there to that check-cashing place across the street, and they will cash it for you. That is the only place that does it, because like I said, we get this all the time, and as long as we stamp the check to show that you came here first, they will cash it."

Nirvana smiled and said, "I would rather do that. I really don't have three to five days."

The lady stamped the check and sent Nirvana on her way. Before Nirvana could leave, the lady stopped her and said, "Wait. Let me put the next one in your name and change your address so you won't have to go through this again."

Chapter 18

Almost Established

It was getting warm outside. Spring was starting to show. Nirvana was getting her check, and her last day with Kikka was approaching. She had given Kikka's mother $250 as an appreciation token for letting her lodge there so that she could leave and start her own life. Nirvana was only seventeen but ready for the world. She was free from captivity and her selfish family who had constantly used her for their own gain. Nirvana was determined to get herself a bank account and an apartment. She still had about four hundred dollars left from her last check, and her next one was due to come in the mail the next day.

Nirvana first went to open a bank account at Trust Credit Union, where they had an account specifically for folks under eighteen. Next, she got on the bus and traveled downtown to go to the mall with shopping on her mind. Then she saw a tall skyscraper-looking building that said Now Leasing on the sign.

She got off the bus and walked over to the building. She talked to the receptionist, who was a middle-aged white lady about forty-five or forty-six. She asked for information about the apartments, and the lady told her that they were studio apartments and they were $340 a month with all utilities included. Nirvana's eyes lit up because she knew that she would be able to afford one with the new cash flow she now had. "Can I see one?" she asked the lady.

The lady said sure and took her up to a corner apartment that was on the fourteenth floor. Nirvana walked in, and it was perfect. It was one huge room that overlooked the city. It had a walk-in closet and a full-size bathroom. A kitchen that had a small refrigerator and stove was hidden behind some doors. Nirvana had the perfect view.

Nirvana looked at the lady and said, "I will take it. What do I need to do?"

The lady said, "Well, let's go back down to the office so that we can talk." They headed back down to the office, and the lady told Nirvana that she needed to be eighteen to sign a lease and needed a steady job to pay the rent. The lady asked her, "How old are you, child?"

"I am seventeen," she replied, "but I get eight hundred twenty-seven dollars a month in social security benefits, so I can afford it. I have nowhere to go, and I can and will pay the rent."

The lady looked at her under-eyed and said, "I am not supposed to do this, but I am going to let you have it. I am going to trust you to do what you say you are going to do. You will need to pay your first rent and deposit before you can move in."

Nirvana went in her purse and counted out $1,020 and gave it to the lady. Nirvana told the lady that she wanted to give her an extra month's worth of rent so that she would feel more secure. The lady looked wowed and handed Nirvana her keys.

As Nirvana was leaving, the lady said to her, "Come back down here to the lobby at about six p.m. That's when I get off. I might have some things for you that you can use."

Nirvana shook her head and went up to her new apartment. She opened the door with her keys, took off her shoes, laid on the hard, bare concrete floor, looking up at the ceilings, smiling and crying at the same time. She was thankful. She knew there was a God. Little did she know that her life was about to begin.

Chapter 19

Just Living

It had been nearly six months, and Nirvana was on her own and loving it. Her apartment was fully furnished with a red sectional couch with a sofa bed, a black dinette set that seated four, and a thirty-two-inch television. Nirvana had also managed to get her wardrobe on point. She had now owned not only a new wardrobe but fourteen pair of stilettos, a few pair of the baldest thigh-high and mid-thigh boots, and two pairs of tennis shoes.

She was right in the heart of Downtown Saint Louis on the fourteenth floor, looking down over the city. She was afraid to explore but knew she had to. It was time for her to get over her self-esteem issues. The sun had just begun to set when she put together a cute ensemble and decided to take a walk in the busy downtown area.

As she was exploring her new neighborhood, she noticed that there were lots of tents along the streets, with tons of people out mingling and holding large cups of liquor. As she approached the steady crowd, she noticed a funnel cake stand and decided to get one. It was the biggest funnel cake she had ever seen, not to mention the best she had ever tasted. It had just the right amount of powdered sugar and a sweet strawberry jam on top. Every bite melted in her mouth almost instantly as she slowly pinched from the circular pattern of the overlapping mass until it was all gone.

"Excuse me, what's your name?" she asked the kind gentleman who had made her funnel cake.

"Jeff. How may I help you?" he asked.

She noticed he had an accent. "I was wondering what type of event this is?" she asked.

"Oh, this is the Taste of Downtown," he replied. "We come all the way from Germany to do this once a year. We go all around the world where they have events like this, and we make good cakes." He winked and smiled at her.

"Oh, OK. Thanks so much for the info." She walked off into the crowd and bumped into her best friend Twyla, whom she had not seen in years.

"Hey, girl!" Twyla said, excited to see her. "Where you been?"

"Oh, just out and about trying to do me," Nirvana said.

"Well, anyways, you should come out on the boulevard tonight with me. I ain't got nobody to go with, and it wasn't meant for me to bump into you for nothing. You can wear what you got on. It's cool," Twyla told her.

Nirvana was nervous about going out with her but accepted the invitation.

Chapter 20

Getting Out

"So where we going on the boulevard?" Nirvana asked Twyla.

"You will see when we get there. We almost there in like five minutes," Twyla said with a devious smirk on her face.

As they approached the boulevard, Twyla found a VIP parking space available and snatched it. They got out of the car and walked about a block up the street. Nirvana noticed a long line outside a building that seemed to be a club. She had never been inside a club before. Her pulse was racing. As they approached, she noticed the name of the club. "Twyla, what kind of name is Club Contagious?"

Twyla replied with a wild, venturous look on her face, "Girl, just what it says. This spot is contagious. Once you get up in herr, you ain't gone wanna leave. Betta yet is some crazy shit up in this piece going on. There some fine-ass fellas up in herr, you will see. I am talking about a whole collection of 'em, and you know I don't discriminate."

Twyla was caramel brown, with chestnut-brown eyes, short naturally blonde hair, and her body was banging. She had the perfect amount of chest, legs, and ass. Twyla proceeded to tell her, "Don't be scared now. Get you a drank and take a deep breath, 'cause it's about ta go down. It's all kinds of folk in here, but they cool." Twyla walked up past the long line and went right on in. She told the cashier that Nirvana was her guest. She always had the hookup every time she went out.

There was one more door they had to enter before actually going into the club, so Nirvana braced herself. She was nervous and didn't really know how to be cool and act normal.

They entered the club, and Nirvana was surprised because it was early and it seemed like everyone in there had popped a sextasy. They were happy people feeling on themselves and touching others. To the left, there was a staircase that led upstairs to a pole and two cages where go-go dancers and half-naked women were dancing. To the right, it was men and women with dog collars and spikes on. She had passed lesbians and obvious homos and more. Then you had your normal folks who were just kicking it in the VIP section, chilling and having a good old time.

Whoever the DJ was, he was jamming, playing a mix of hip-hop with rave music. Nirvana didn't really care for the rave music, but it was something for her to get used to. The lights were going crazy, almost blinding her. She thought to herself that she should have worn a pair of shades. She looked at Twyla and said, "Girl, you wasn't lying. Now I see why it's called Contagious. I like it."

Twyla turned and said, "I told you this shit is off the chainz, right? You gone be back. There ain't neva any drama going down here. The owners, Kent and Ted, ain't having it. I am gone introduce you to them later. They hella cool."

Nirvana went to the bar while Twyla followed. Nirvana asked the bartender for a Sprite and lime.

"Naaaunnn," Twyla said, rolling her eyes and neck in harmony with each other. "Girl, you didn't come in here to have an ol' janky-ass Sprite. I can buy you a Sprite later with my food stamps. You know I get plenty.

"Hey, bartender, give me two tall glasses of Alizé with light ice, please. Girl, it's da weekend, and you hanging with me. You about to be on one. You need to live a little. It's time to crack the eggshell wide open and sizzle a little."

The bartender handed them their drinks, and they walked back over to the VIP lounge where they run into Ted, one of the owners, and Twyla introduced them.

Ted was tall, about six foot three and had medium brown skin. His body was firmly built, like a knight with shining armor.

Nirvana had peeped at his shoe size, which looked to be a size 12. She had always wondered if what they said was true about men with large feet. He was undeniably a true gentleman with a pleasant and respectable persona. "Hey, Ted, this my girl Nirvana. She don't get out that much. Make sure you take care of her if she comes without me."

Ted smiled and reached out to shake Nirvana's hand and said in a solid baritone voice, "Hello, young lady. I hope you enjoy yourself tonight." He had slightly full lips—the kind that ended with a smirk at the end.

Nirvana was instantly captivated with his tone of voice; it was deep and gentle. His voice sent chills up her spine, and she somewhat felt weak in the knees. "I will, and thank you. I will be back," she said.

As Ted dismissed himself, Nirvana followed him with her eyes as he went behind the bar to check the totals for the night.

"Girl, I know he fine," Twyla said as she snapped her fingers in front of Nirvana's face. "They crazy thing is, girl, he single too. I always said to myself, 'How can a man be so damn fine and be single?'"

Yeah, he is, Nirvana thought, still thinking about all his features.

"OK, well, let's get our party on," Twyla said. "I wanna leave before it gets too packed, and I'm hungry. I would get something from here, but they look too damn sweaty all in here for me to eat." She laughed out loud.

Nirvana could tell the Alizé was making her feel a bit too good. Nirvana was babysitting her drink but was slowly sipping. The music continued to play while they both ended up staying and dancing the night away.

Chapter 21

The Call

The alarm clock in Nirvana's apartment had just gone off, and her phone was ringing off the hook while her pager was beeping continuously. She sat up in her bed quickly to get her thoughts together. She pushed the alarm so that it could stop beeping. She answered the phone while looking at her pager. "Hello," she said.

"What you doing, NV?" the voice said on the other line. NV was short for Nirvana, and that's what most of her close friends and family called her.

"Oh, nothing. Just woke up, Aunty," she answered. It was her aunt Parice, one of her mother's older sisters. Every now and then, Parice would call Nirvana and check up on her and see if she wanted to hang out.

"Awww, OK. Well, I am so damn mad right now," Parice went on to say. "I am gone end up having to get another car, or I am gone have to start sucking some dick, and you know Aunty don't know how, but it's time I learn. I done paid these car people $1,400 to fix my car. I ain't ever had to pay that much to fix my car. It's definitely time to sale some pussy. I can set up shop behind Quick Trip because you know it's going to be a quick in and out. You know I got that good shit too. I can make it fort, clap, and more. Whateva they want, I can do. I need some money." Patrice told this to Nirvana while laughing uncontrollably.

"Aunty, you so crazy," Nirvana said, laughing so hard tears were in her eyes.

56

Parice was a single woman with no kids, about forty-five, and was one of the most hilarious people to be around. Parice was very organized and so clean that she had white carpets in her house. If you didn't know her, you would really think what she was saying was true. The truth was that everyone in the family said she was a virgin. She had never even seen a penis close up because she was too scared of catching a disease. Parice would say some of the most unexpected things to get your day started. For sure, she had just made Nirvana's day.

"You wanna hang out?" Parice asked Nirvana.

"No, not today, Aunty. I got to try to find me a job. I need a li'l extra income coming in. You know I would, Aunty, if I could."

"Well, OK, li'l girl, I guess I will go find some dick to suck by myself. I was gone see if you wanted to learn with me. Or maybe you could show me the ropes?" Parice said, laughing so extremely hard she could barely get her words out. "I will talk to you later."

"OK, Aunty." Nirvana hung the phone up. Her eyes were still tearing up because she couldn't believe what she had just woken up to. It was a good thing though her aunt Parice had just made her morning.

Chapter 22

JOB (Jumping on the Boulevard)

Nirvana had slipped on some baggy jeans, a green tie-dye tank top, and tennis to go around the city to look for work. She didn't feel like dressing up or doing her hair, so she wrapped her hair in a scarf and kept it moving.

She was still trying to get her mojo back from the weekend escapade with Twyla. She decided to catch the bus down on the boulevard. Since her brother Vadyme lived near that way, she could stop by his house for some family time. As she was riding the bus, she was passing all types of malls and restaurants where she knew she could have easily gotten employed. For some reason, she decided to stay on the bus for about two more blocks where she approached many of the nightclubs that was on the boulevard.

After going to Club Contagious with Twyla, Nirvana's gut yearned for something more exciting. She rang the bell on the bus so that the bus driver could let her off and began to walk up and down the boulevard. She was really just exploring until she heard a voice say, "Hello, young lady." She was startled and hesitated to look back, and she kept walking. She heard the voice again attempt to get her attention and say "Excuse me, miss." The voice was deep and endearing. It sent chills up her spine. She slowly turned around to notice that it was Ted, the owner of Contagious, with another gentleman she had not met. Her stomach dropped as she walked back toward Ted.

"Hello," she said as she approached him.

"Hi! I was just trying to give you a flyer to come check out our club this weekend," Ted told her.

She looked at him but realized that he didn't recognize her. She took the flyer and started to walk off before she heard his voice demand her return.

"Hey! Hey, what's your name?" he said as he took a few steps to catch up with her. It didn't take him long to catch up because his legs were long like a giraffe's.

She turned and said, "NV."

He looked at her face for a while and said, "You know, you have such a gorgeous face. Your cheekbones sit at just the right height, your eyes are big and bright, and your smile is bright like a diamond."

Nirvana blushed, but she was insecure because all her life, she had been told she was ugly. She never had anyone instill in her that she was pretty. Nor had anyone ever given her that many compliments. She had her guards up. "You think I'm pretty? How can you think that? Look at me: I have on the baggy clothes, and my hair isn't even done," she started to point out to Ted. Nirvana immediately started to down herself. She continued to find reasons why Ted shouldn't find her attractive.

Ted smiled with a slight smirk and told her none of that mattered. "I am looking at your face. It's beautiful. If you can look flawless like this, I can only imagine how you would look when you are put together. I like it," he told her.

Nirvana was still not convinced but went with the flow.

"What brings you down here to the boulevard?" he asked.

"I was just scoping things out, looking for some work," she told Ted.

Ted put his hand on his chin and asked her, "Have you ever thought about dancing?"

Nirvana was shocked. "Dancing how? Like ballet or tap dancing?" she said, even though she really knew what he meant.

"Ha-ha! You're so funny." Ted laughed. "Come to my office with me, and we can sit down and talk a bit more instead of being out in this hot sun."

Nirvana followed him about a block up the street to Club Contagious, back to his office, where she took a seat on the all-white leather chaise that was in Ted's office.

Ted sat down and said. "You are gorgeous. I never had any intentions of asking you such a thing, but a young lady like yourself to come down here looking for work gave me nothing but open opportunity.

"If you are interested in dancing, we have private parties here on Fridays and Sundays. We hire about three to four girls, and they get a flat rate of $100 plus their tips. You have to get naked, but we do require you to at least get topless. I am not here to pressure you. It's all up to you. It's quick and good money. You will only have to dance off two songs. That's less than ten minutes."

Nirvana thought about it for a few minutes then agreed to take the job. Ever since she had been to Club Contagious, she had been wanting to feel more of that kind of excitement. She had never danced before except in her mirror at home in her bathroom. Her adrenaline was rushing, and she was ready for a new challenge.

Ted looked at her with his perfect lips and said, "Very well, then. I will see you this weekend. Now you need to go get you some sexy dance wear. There is a shop on the east end of the boulevard called Luqy Girl Novelties. Ask for Shanna, tell her I sent you."

"OK, Ted, thanks."

"See you this weekend at nine o'clock sharp," he interrupted.

Chapter 23

The Dance

"Girl, what the hell is this?" Twyla yelled out as she went through Nirvana, shopping bags revealing the exotic clothes that were in the bag. "No, you ain't gone wear this, and where you suppose to wear it to? Don't you know that if your momma knew you were wearing this type of shit, she would be turning in her grave?" Twyla exclaimed, but she was excited at the same time.

"Girl, I didn't get to tell you, but I got a job as a dancer down at Contagious last week. I ran into Ted on the boulevard, and the crazy thing is, I don't even think he knew it was me. I mean, it was dark in the club that night," she said to Twyla.

"For real? That is crazy. So what's your stage name?" Twyla asked.

"My stage name?"

"Yes! You can't go out dancing with your real name. Duhh!" Twyla yelled.

"I don't know. What do you think?" Nirvana heeded for advice from her friend.

Twyla thought for a few minutes and said, "How about Choclik? It's different and unique, and you chocolate too."

"I like, I like, I like! Ohhhh, Mafaasaa," Nirvana joked.

"Say it again," Twyla said as they laughed about the name that they had come up with. "Well, I do have one question for you."

"What?"

"How you gone make it clap? 'Cause you ain't got no ass!" Twyla said, bursting out into laughter right afterward.

Nirvana was really self-conscious about her butt. She was always told that she had an ass like a white girl, that it was flat like a pancake, and that it was a shake with no shake. It didn't bother her when Twyla teased. They had been friends for such a long time. She looked at Twyla and said, "I may not have a perfectly round hump like you, but where there is a will, there is a way."

The weekend had finally come, and it was time for Nirvana to perform for the first time. She was nervous and anxious at the same time. She had been practicing routines in front of her mirror at home and had built a bit of confidence up, but she still needed reassurance. As she sat in the dressing room with more advanced dancers, she was greeted by a dancer named Yummi.

Yummi was a full-bodied woman. Her skin tone was golden caramel brown. She stood at about five foot three without heels, and her measurements were 34-25-42. "Hey, youngling," Yummi said to Nirvana. "So this your first time dancing?"

Nirvana replied, "Yeah, and I am scared as hell. I have never done this before. How will I know they will like me? And I don't have a real big butt like you." Nirvana holding her head down.

Yummi sat down directly in front of Nirvana and said to her, "Sweetheart, you are beautiful, and don't never let anyone else tell you different. You may not have the biggest ass or the biggest breast, but it's all about how you use them. And as far as them liking you, when them dollas start pouring, you will know. The muthafuccas here easy. You ain't got to do much. They just wanna see some fine women and go home and fuck the shit out of their wives, and most of them even come with their girlfriends and wives. You don't have nothing to be afraid of. Just imagine you are in front of a mirror, alone at home and dancing all by yourself. Girl, as far as not havin' a big butt, I can show you how to make it clap just with what you got before I go out on my set."

Nirvana's eyes lit up, and she asked Yummi, "Can you? Please?"

Yummi instructed her to get onto the floor on all fours, with her legs spread apart, and instructed her to practice moving her glute muscles. She told Nirvana to experiment with her legs at different widths apart to find what makes her butt move more or less. She also showed her how to do the same thing standing on only her legs in stilettos too. Yummi smiled and said, "There you go. You getting it. Keep doing this, and your ass gone be moving out of control before you know it. It ain't all about how much ass you got. Practice at home too.

"OK, it's time for me to go on stage. Good luck, see you in a bit!" she said while she gave Nirvana a wink.

There was a knock on the dressing room door that startled Nirvana because she was practicing the new booty dance she had just learned. "Ummm, who is it?" she yelled out.

"It's Ted," the voice said behind the door.

"Come in," she replied.

Ted slowly opened the door and walked in, and you could tell by his face that he was impressed with what graced his sight. "Absolutely stunning!" he complimented. "I was just coming back to check on you and to see what you want to dance off of? You can choose up to three songs, but you only have to do two," he informed her.

Nirvana said quickly, "I was thinking about Master P's 'How You Do That There,' 'Something for the People,' and 'My Love Is da Shhh.'"

Ted smiled and nodded. "OK. It seems like you have your mind made up. I will let the DJ know, and you're up next. Oh, what name do you want to come out to?" he asked.

"Choclik," she said as she rolled her tongue in harmony with the annunciation of the name she and Twyla had made up.

He smiled again and shook his head as he walked out of the dressing room, smiling, saying to himself, "Choclik. Cute."

Nirvana looked in the mirror to check her flawless makeup and hair before she went out to dance. She hurriedly peeked out the door to watch Yummi finish up her performance. She noticed that there wasn't a dance pole and realized that this type of dancing was all about skill and captivating your audience. Nirvana was adorned with a cute, one-piece, long-sleeved sequined gold thong getup that had a sequined bra and pair of gold shorts to match. She was feeling a bit more confident and ready to showcase her skills.

"Coming to the stage now is a newcomer," she heard the DJ say. "She is sexy, desirable, and Choclik!"

The first song was Master P, and Nirvana strutted out into the lights and imagined herself at home, dancing in the mirror. She bent over in front of her audience, showing off her birthday suit. She could hear the crowd screaming and yelling for more, which made her even more confident. She got her audience's attention by clapping her hands in harmony with the music, yelling to the crowd, "How you do that therr?"

A gentleman stood up in the crowd with a wad of cash, saying, "Damn, baby, come over here."

She slowly worked her way through the crowd, giving innocent and quick lap dances until she reached the gentleman yelling for her to come his way. Security guards, with buckets collecting her cash as it was thrown into the air, followed her through the crowd as she made her way over to the gentleman that was yelling for her to come his way. When she made it to him, he showered her with continuous bills.

Nirvana didn't have to worry about picking up her money because there were security guards with flashlights and baskets following her, picking her bills up. As the next track began to play, she worked her way back in front of the crowd and did a split on a young man who had lain on the floor holding a twenty dollar bill in his hand. She grabbed the money and continued to do her thing. The crowd was cheering and roaring for more. As her set came to an end, a guy in the crowd stood up and yelled, "We still got money! Dance one more song."

Nirvana looked at the DJ and gave him the cue to play another cut. Nirvana was really feeling herself.

The DJ played R. Kelly and Biggie Smalls' "Fucking You Tonight," and it was on and popping. The crowd continued to roar like never before as Nirvana shook her booty across the crowd. When her set was finally over, she went into the dressing room and sat down with a huge smile on her face. The bouncers shortly came in and gave two baskets full of money. She looked at the money and started to count it immediately. She had more large bills than small ones. She had counted out more than $900. She was excited and couldn't believe she had made nearly a thousand dollars in less than twenty minutes.

Chapter 24

Addiction

It had now been Nirvana's second month on the job. Working only two nights a week, she was a beast. The money was fast, quick, and easy. She still had to find something to do during the week as well. She applied for a job at a local boutique called Havana Nights in the downtown area, blocks from where she lived, and was hired almost immediately. She chose to work at a boutique because she could use the unique fashion to spoof up her dance outfits when she danced at Club Contagious. She also received a 30 percent discount on her purchases. What more could a girl ask for? She was nearly bringing in three grand a week. Most of her money went into separate checking and savings accounts because she wanted to buy a car. She wasn't in a rush for wheels yet. She loved taking the bus and walking, because it kept her legs well-defined and toned. Even her booty started to firm up and get some curves. She was addicted to money now, and nothing was going to stop her from getting it.

Chapter 25

Chicago

Nirvana had just made it to Club Contagious, rushing in to make her set on time. She was running late because the bus had a mechanical failure and she had to wait for another one. As she rushed to put on her costume, she was approached by Yummi.

"Girl, what you been up to?" Yummi asked.

Nirvana replied, "Just getting this money. I been working here, and I got another job at a boutique near my home."

"Oh, that's what's up!" Yummi smiled as she hurried and asked Nirvana if she wanted to go to Chicago.

"Chicago!" Nirvana yelled. "I ain't ever been out of the Lou all like that. What's in Chicago?"

"Weeeeell, there's this guy named Ein. He always taking me and my girls to Chi Town to make some extra bucks. Last time I went, I made nearly six Gs in a weekend. You should go. It normally is like ten girls, and we go have fun. Our hotel is paid for, all our meals, and he gives us two hundred dollars upfront just for going. He will give that to you before you even actually go. But I am telling you, you should go. Didn't you say earlier when you first started that you were all about your money? Well, if that is the case, you need to be in the place."

"When are we supposed to go?" Nirvana asked.

"Next weekend. Just tell Ted you taking off. He ain't gone trip. He got plenty of girls and trust they would appreciate the money. Besides, this chump change ain't anything compared to what you about to get out here in Chi Town. Trust and believe, sweetie," Yummi replied.

Nirvana's cheekbones were glowing as they were lifted to its highest height, and her lips stretched from ear to ear as she agreed to go on this trip with Yummi. Everything sounded like sweet, smooth jazz music to Nirvana's ears, but she had no idea what she was really getting herself into.

The upcoming weekend was approaching, and Nirvana was ready. All she could think about was being on stage with bright lights while money poured all over her. She thought that it was going to be a come up. After she finished daydreaming, she called Ted to tell him she needed the weekend off. When she called Ted, she was surprised for him to ask her to stop by if it wasn't any trouble. She hurried up and put on some clothes and rushed to go see what Ted needed to see her for. She was hoping he wasn't going to fire her. All she could think about was what she could have done wrong.

She finally arrived at Club Contagious and went to Ted's office. "Hello, Ted, you wanted to see me?" she asked.

"Yes, have a seat," he said.

Every time he spoke, chills went up her spine. His voice was very alluring to her, and it did something to her. "OK, about what?"

"Well, I never really get into other folks' business, but I hear you are taking a trip with Yummi this weekend?"

"Ummm, yeah, she asked me to go. She said I can make a whole lot of money. And you know I am all for it."

"Ummhuhh," he said as his strong hand caressed his chin as if he was thinking. He took a deep breath and began to tell Nirvana that, for one, she was very pretty and attractive and she should not let the sound of money ruin her before she had a chance to start her life. "I am not going to tell you what to do. I just want you to be careful. Yummi is a good person, but not all things she indulges in are good for her or you. Just be smart about the decisions you make. Money isn't everything," he told her.

Nirvana held her head down and said, "Thank you, Ted, for being concerned, but I will like to see for myself." While she was sitting on the chaise couch Ted had in his office, he got out of his seat from behind his desk and sat next to her.

"You are very beautiful," he said. "I have been wanting to tell you that for a long time."

Nirvana looked at him, almost melted, while she asked, "How many of these girls you tell that?"

He replied and said, "Only three, including you. I never dealt with any of my girls before. I always tell them they look nice because it keeps their spirits up. There is just something about you." He touched her face gently. Nirvana started to feel weird in a good way; Ted's voice already was too much for her to handle in the first place.

"Can I kiss you?" Ted asked her.

Nirvana had never been kissed or touched in such a way by any man before. She gave him the OK as she thought he was going to kiss her lips; instead he kissed her forehead very gently. Ted could tell she was a virgin, and he wanted first dibs but knew he had to take his time. His intentions were not to harm her in any way. In fact, he wanted to be with her. After he kissed her forehead, he sat behind her and started to massage her shoulders and neck while whispering in her ear. "Be careful on this trip. You are my diamond. If you need anything, call me. I don't care what hour it is. Call me, OK?"

She nodded for she could not speak. She was relaxed and outdone by what had just happened. Her body craved for more, but Ted left her sitting on the chaise as he dismissed himself.

Nirvana stood up with shaky legs and headed out to get the next bus home so that she could pack her bags for the weekend getaway.

When she got home, Twyla was waiting for her in the downstairs lobby. "Girl, where you been? You didn't have to work today." Twyla asked.

"Yeah, I know, girl. I had to go handle something down at the club. It's all good now. I am supposed to be going to Chicago with one of the dancers at the club this weekend to dance. I will be back Sunday night. I have to make this money, honey," she told Twyla.

"Well, do what you do, just be careful. I don't wanna have to fuck nobody up, you hear me?"

"Yeah, girl, I hear you. I am gone be all right though."

Chapter 26

The Drive

Friday had finally arrived, and Nirvana was anxious about her trip to Chi Town. She grabbed her weekend bag and hopped on the bus to go down to the boulevard to meet Yummi and Ein. When she arrived, there were about seven vehicles parked in front of the club. There stood Yummi and Ein. Ein was tall and handsome. He had a pimp vibe to him, which made Nirvana have second thoughts about the trip, but she still decided to go because she had never been out of the city before. "Hey, girl, I am ready!" she said to Yummi.

"I hope you are! Come on, let me introduce you to Ein. Ein, this girl Choclik I was telling you about."

"Hey, what's up, Choclik?" Ein greeted as if he was turned on by the way Nirvana's stage name was pronounced. He reached to shake her hand.

As Nirvana pulled her hand away from Ein, she realized that he had put two hundred-dollar bills in her hand. Nirvana was grateful and took the money and put it in the Chanel purse she had just purchased from the Brookville Plaza Mall a few weekends ago.

"OK, are y'all ready to hit the road? Well, hop aboard!" Ein instructed everyone.

Nirvana scoped out all the cars lined up in front of Club Contagious. She was trying to decide if she wanted to ride in the Navigator with Yummi or take her chances riding in one of the BMWs with someone she didn't know.

"Come on, girl! Ain't no point in riding with them. You ain't quite ready for that ride. Ride with me and the girls!" Yummi screamed.

Nirvana jumped into the Navigator and sat in the first row seat with Yummi. As she looked around, folks were reaching out, greeting her and introducing themselves to her. There were about four other girls, including her and Yummi, with two fine-ass guys riding with them.

"Hey, my name is Earl," the driver looked back and said.

"Hey, and I'm Sam!" the other guy said.

Nirvana was nervous but felt a jolt of adrenaline rushing through her veins. Chi Town was a four hour drive, so she decided that she might as well get comfortable since everyone else had. Everyone was pouring drinks while passing some of the best weed she had ever inhaled.

"You smoke?" one of the girls asked Nirvana.

"From time to time," she answered.

"Well, here, girl, take a pull. By the way, my name is Gayeilla," the girl said to Nirvana.

Nirvana took the joint and started to involve herself in the ongoing circle of smoke. Gayeilla offered her a drink too, but she passed because she was not fond of "I don't know what hell is in that cup" type of drinks. As the noise of the crowded SUV started to settle down, Nirvana gazed out the window, thinking whether she made a bad decision. Everyone had fallen asleep except for Gayeilla, who had made her way into the passenger seat next to Earl. It was dark, but Nirvana could see the silhouette of Gayeilla leaning across toward Earl. As she focused closely, she realized that Gayeilla was giving Earl some major head work. That was her first time seeing anyone give a blow job, and that also explained why Earl kept speeding up then slowing down in constant small spurts of speed while he was driving.

Earl noticed Nirvana was watching and winked at her through the rearview mirror. Nirvana closed her eyes quickly while acting as if she was asleep. She had started to get a woozy feeling in her stomach because she knew that if they were behaving like this on the road, there was no telling what else they were capable of when they were to arrive in Chicago.

Chapter 27

The Wait

It was about 9:00 p.m. when they finally arrived in Chicago. The streets were all lit up, people were walking the streets and enjoying their strolls, and even the homeless looked as if they were enjoying asking passersby for change. As they drove the Magnificent Mile, they approached a very high-profile hotel. When Nirvana got out of the Burgan Navigator, she walked into the lobby of the hotel and noticed bellhop men awaiting their arrival.

She was wowed and couldn't believe her eyes. She had never seen such a sensory of bliss. There were pearl marbled floors with navy-blue leather winged back chairs with charming sparkling chandeliers. This hotel had nothing but artistic charm. The atmosphere had a friendly vibe that put you right in tune with the city's energy. Nirvana was in love.

"Come on, girl! Snap out of it. I told you they were gone treat us real good. Come on! Wait till you see this penthouse we about to be in. Three full bedrooms in this bish. Full kitchen, ahhh, Jacuzzi—the works, baby! Don't be scared. Enjoy yourself," Yummi told her, smiling and rushing to get to the penthouse because she had to really use the bathroom.

Yummi opened the door to the penthouse suite and rushed to the first restroom she saw. Nirvana was scoping out the view. They were on the eighteenth floor of the hotel and had an awesome view of the Mile. She felt like she was in paradise. She thought to herself the sky is the limit.

Nirvana went into one of the bedrooms and unpacked her things while she waited for Yummi to get out of the shower. She knew they were getting ready to hit the streets because they were invited to a party on a yacht down on the Chicago Harbor. Nirvana decided to wear her turquoise leather leopard-print invisible wedge boots with five-inch heels by Bobbie Jae and an all-white short minidress with cowl neck that hung low to where you can see her cleavage and open back. Her accessories were several different shades of gray while she owned a Swarovski crystal clutch to make her whole ensemble pop.

"Girl, you looking nice in that ice," Yummi complimented as she came into the room from showering to put on her clothes.

Nirvana accepted the compliment by saying "Thank you." She walked away like she was going to be the baddest bish on the scene. Her confidence was building up, and she felt unstoppable.

As she and Yummi headed down to the lobby to join the others for their ride to the yacht party, they noticed three white stretch limousines out in front of the hotel. Ein came off the elevator and told everyone to find a seat in one of the limos. They both get in since the doors were already opened for them. Nirvana looked at Yummi under-eyed and asked, "This must be some kind of party."

Yummi looked at her deep in the eyes and said, "You ain't seen nothing yet. Wait till we get on this boat! Girl, your eye cherry is about to get popped, 'cause none of this is for virgin eyes."

Chapter 28

Party Yacht

They were now in line waiting to board the yacht. Nirvana was anxious, but Yummi was calm and collected because this wasn't anything new to her. Yummi was used to all the bright lights and the street life.

Nirvana boarded the yacht while a gentleman held her hand so she wouldn't fall. *It feels good to be treated like a lady,* she thought. The yacht was decked out with all kinds of buffet bars in almost every room she had peeked into. There were two bars with nothing but the best wines, cognacs, and vodkas.

When she went downstairs to the lower level of the yacht, there were women and men walking around in the nude. Some were in really sexy lingerie, others were stark naked, and then you had Nirvana. She felt so appalled. Although Nirvana didn't really like what she was seeing, it was still surreal to her. Yummi was sure right. Her eye cherry had just been popped. She went back upstairs to find Yummi. Nirvana was very upset.

Yummi was cuddled with some guy she probably had only known five minutes. Nirvana grabbed Yummi's arm and yanked her from the gentlemen. "I need to talk to you now!" she demanded Yummi.

Yummi had been drinking all day and was tipsy, so her body was flung from the force of Nirvana's pulls. "What's up, Choclik? What's all this about?" Yummi asked.

Nirvana looked at her with an eye of fury. "You know what I'm talking about. All these naked men and women walking downstairs. I go downstairs, and I see two women eating each other's sushi. And I just saw one of the biggest dicks in my life. It was so beautiful. But I am still mad! Bitch, you didn't tell me about this! I thought we were coming to dance! You could have told me about this beforehand."

Yummi stood straight and said, "OK, I am sorry I didn't tell you. But I knew you wouldn't come if I had. Always remember, in this game, nothing is what it seems to be. I ain't trying to turn you out, but you always talking about how you about your money and shit. I thought I would broaden your horizons. This is where the real money at. You are your own person. I exposed you to this life, this is the real world, sweetie, but you can make your own decisions. What you don't want to do is your choice.

"But it's some folks here that will take you shopping just because it's nothing. Sometimes they just want your presence. It's not always a sexual thing at these parties. It's just all about what you like want. The downstairs is for folks that have some wild sexual fetishes and the upstairs is for the grown, sexy, casual, and discreet folks. So now it's on you. Not me. Make you some money, that all I got to say. I knew you wasn't going to be ready for that ride. It's truly for the grown folks. If you wanna be just grown, then take your ass downstairs. If you wanna be grown and classy, I think you get the picture."

Yummi swung her long curly weave and walked off, leaving Nirvana standing alone on the balcony of the yacht. Nirvana waited in quiet thought while the wind blew against her face.

Chapter 29

Approached Rapidly

Nirvana decided to hang out upstairs. The downstairs thing was a bit too much for her. She played it safe. As she sat at the bar and sipped on a glass of Rémy, she was approached by a tall fine gentleman. He was about six feet four, dark skinned. His frame was like a finely sculpted statue. He was a sophisticated gangster type of guy. His grill was on ice, but he was dressed like a professional businessman that carried a small briefcase around with him. To Nirvana, his style was different but edgy, and she was enticed by it.

He sat next to her and whispered in her ear, asking her with his smooth Jamaican accent why she was so beautiful and attending such a party. While he asked her, he caressed the side of her neck.

Nirvana was instantly put under the spell of his cologne, and the smell of it had her crave his venom. "I was invited by a friend. This is my first time here," she replied.

"Huuummm, I see. Look, I am not trying to disrespect you or anything. But you are just stunning. I love your smile, and you also seem like you might need some company, so my question is, can we hang out tonight and maybe even tomorrow? I will show you around the city. Let's just hang out here, walk around and get to know each other. Or if you want, we can go to my condo on the other side of town. You will love it. I just need some company tonight," he explained.

Nirvana was so shocked, but she took him up on the offer. She didn't really feel in her comfort zone, so she went and found Yummi to inform her she would meet her back at the hotel later. "OK, girl, I will see you. Have fun. You got my number, and I got yours," Yummi said while waving her off.

"Oh, my! I didn't even get your name. I am just leaving with a stranger," she asked, laughing.

"I was just thinking the same thing. My name is Georgjae, but you can call me Jae'," he told her.

"I'm Nirvana," she replied with a cute, bashful smirk.

Jae' had a Lincoln Town Car waiting as they exited the yacht. They got into the car and rode off into the night. When they arrived at his condo, they indulged in flirtatious conversation while drinking wine, and then later they passed out on the couch.

The next morning, Nirvana woke up to find that Jae' was missing from her side. She looked around while stumbling through the house. As she went into one of the bedrooms, she heard water running. When she went into the bathroom, there was Jae' standing there with a smile on his face. Jae' was partially nude with a French terry cloth wrapped around his waist. His structured chest and long, narrow torso was glistening as if he had rubbed oil all over himself. She was instantly turned on.

"Good morning! I drew you a bath with lavender oil and rose pedals. Go ahead and get yourself together so that we can catch breakfast and stroll the Mile before you have to leave me."

Nirvana was pleased and engulfed herself in the lavender bath while Jae' watched her. He took a sponge and helped wash her flawless skin clean. This all felt great to Nirvana. She was still a bit nervous but went with the flow. After she exited the tub, she went into the room and sat on the bed, and Jae' rubbed her down with lavender and sage oils. The aroma filled the room and also put Nirvana in a relaxed state. After Jae' finished rubbing her down with oils, he went to the closet to retrieve a dress, sandals, scarf, and a panties and bra set from Victoria's Secret.

As she put on the bra set, Jae' watched with awe. "You are absolutely gorgeous," he told Nirvana. "I hope you don't mind, but I sent my driver to go pick you up a few things to wear since you were not going to be going back to your hotel soon."

Nirvana replied. "Awwww! I feel so grateful. No one has ever done this for me before. Thank you."

They finally made it to a cozy restaurant on the Mile, where they enjoyed brunch and mimosas. After breakfast, he took Nirvana on a shopping spree. She had shopped at Top Shop, Zara's, and many more local boutiques along the Magnificent Mile.

Nirvana felt great but knew all this came with a price. "Ummm, Jae', can I ask you a question? Why are you doing all of this for me? Do you expect anything from me?" Nirvana wanted everything that was given to her but was afraid of what Jae' might want from her in return.

He looked at her and told her, "I want you. I am a gentleman, and I don't expect anything from you, but I do want you. There is something about the way you carry yourself, and I like it. I can have anyone I want, but I choose to show you a good time, if you let me. All I ask is that you just go with the flow and relax. You are in good hands, I promise," he said.

As the day came to an end, they both went back to his condo, where he caressed her mind with everything she had always wanted to hear. As she lay on the bed, he slowly took her shoes off and massaged her feet and legs. He could feel her trembling, and it turned him on. He slowly took his hand and rubbed up her thighs then took off her dress. Nirvana tried to stop him, but he whispered in her ear, "Just relax and let me please you." Her body gave in as she lay back on the bed. Jae' took a pillow wedge and placed it under her butt so that her innocent vagina was propped up into the air. He slowly rubbed it while he watched her body jolt vigorously out of control.

Nirvana had never been touched this way, and it felt so good to her soul. Jae' continued to pleasure her while he kissed the rest of her body. As he began to enter her, she moaned uncontrollably. He moved his manhood in and out slowly because he realized she was still a virgin. As he pleasured himself with her innocent body, they both came to climax and fell asleep.

Chapter 30

Home Sweet Home

Nirvana was now back home in her own bed. She had enjoyed herself in Chicago. She had lost her virginity to a man that she knew she would never see again. She had come back with so many gifts and money. Jae' had bought her all kinds of clothes, purses, and shoes. She had never felt so good. Not to mention she wasn't a virgin anymore.

"Hello," she said as she picked up her phone to find it was Yummi on the other end. "Hey, girl, I was just checking on you to see what you were up to and to see if you enjoyed yourself?"

"Yeah, I had a wonderful time. Jae' treated me really nice."

"See? I told you. It's all about who you meet. You lucked out and found someone that knew how to wine and dine. Like I told you before, most of the time, when you attend those types of parties, that is what all the men are looking for. 'Cause believe me, they either be married or in a relationship," Yummi explained. Yummi continued to ramble on. "Anyway, girl, I was calling to tell you about Gayeilla. Gayeilla was a simple white girl who lived in Liberty Trailer Park and had three kids by three different black men and had wanted a better life for her and her family. During the trip to Chicago, she rambled on about how she was going to come up, and when she got back home, she was going to take her kids shopping and move to a better place. Girl! This bitch made nearly ten racks. She ain't got any shame in her game.

"Girl, Ein had to go get her ass from the yacht the next day. Her stank booty ass was getting it in. There was a room on the lower level where they were doing all kinds of stuff, and she was in that room, sucking, fucking, and giving hand jobs at the same damn time." Yummi giggled. "And she ain't have no shame in her game. There were men lined up outside the yacht waiting to screw her."

"Whoa!" Nirvana interrupted. "That's why I saw all those guys standing in line that night? Wow!"

Yummi began to proceed. "Anyhow, she was literally fucking till six o'clock in the morning. The word is she was literally bleeding."

"Ihhhh!" Nirvana said with a look of disgust on her face. "Well, girl, I guess that's how they get it in nowadays."

"I guess so, but I know one thing—ain't no vinegar bath gone help her. Her pussball has to be beat up out the box!" Yummi said, laughing.

"Unnnn," Nirvana said on the other end of the phone while laughing so hard tears were in her eyes. "Well, girl, I will talk to you later."

Chapter 31

Back to Work

"Hey, Ted, how are you?" Nirvana asked as she walked to the dressing room.

"How are you?" he replied as he followed behind her. "How was your trip?"

"Oh, Ted, it was just fine. It was some crazy stuff going on, but I kept clear of all of that," she told him.

When she walked into the dressing room, Ted came in behind her and locked the door. "I missed you," he told her while pinning her up against the wall and pressing himself into her.

"I can tell, but you know I have to go out and dance in the next few minutes, Ted."

"Baby, just let me taste you. I have been craving you since you left."

Nirvana relaxed as she let him take control. Her hormones were now like a tornado that had just touched the ground. He lifted her up and sat her on the countertop and opened her legs, ripping off her thong, and went to work. She could not get Jae' off her mind. As Ted pleasured her, she trembled and moaned. Nirvana had now had two sexual encounters. Her hormones were starting to catch up with her. Now she was craving sexual bliss all the time.

It was now time for her to dance, and someone was knocking at the dressing room door. How was she going to explain that she was locked in the dressing room with Ted? She thought. She hurried and put on her costume while Ted sat in one of the chairs, as if they were having a serious conversation. She opened the door, and Yummi came in.

"Dang! Why y'all in here with the door locked and shish? Well, it ain't my business. I'm just saying."

Ted and Nirvana got up and walked out of the dressing room without any comments.

It had been nearly two years since Nirvana had been working at Club Contagious. She had decided to make it clear with Ted that she didn't want to do dance forever and that she was giving him a two-week notice. Ted didn't want to see her leave, because he knew it would mean that what they shared would be over. Nirvana continued to perform as she prepared to work full-time at Havana Nights.

One evening on her way home, she met a young man named Devonta in the lobby of her apartments. Devonta was about five foot eight, with a butterscotch-toned completion. It looked as if his skin had been kissed by the sun. His smile was something amazing. When he smiled, it looked like his cheeks had been pierced. He was not put together well. His shoes looked like they were talking to him. He drove a small 1990 Volkswagen bug, but he had a very pleasant personality. Even though he was not Nirvana's type, she tended not to pay attention to his outer appearance. He asked her if she needed help with anything, since her hands were full of bags. She told him no and proceeded to go into her apartment building while he held the door for her.

"Thank you," she said as she headed toward the elevator. She went up to her apartment and crashed instantly. She was very tired and worn out from working two jobs.

The next day Twyla called her and asked her if she wanted to go to a stage play called *How to Treat a Woman Right*. Nirvana had told her that she was going with a guy she had met over the weekend, and he had a friend for her. Nirvana agreed to take her up on the offer.

"Great! I am glad you do. His friend is a really nice guy. I will tell you, he is not what you are used to dating, but remember to try to look past the outside so you can see what's on the inside. Besides, it's just a date. Whoever said you were going to fall in love?" Twyla joked with Nirvana.

"Girl, whatever, as long as he got money to pay for me some food. 'Cause I can't mess with no broke niggas. I need that moola. You feel me?" she said to Twyla.

"Yeah, yeah, whatever! We will pick you up tomorrow at seven o'clock. The play starts at eight o'clock sharp, so be ready and wear something nice."

Chapter 32

Date Night

Nirvana was waiting for Twyla and their dates to arrive, so she waited in the lobby of her apartment building. When they arrived, Twyla introduced her blind date. Nirvana realized that was Devonta whom she had just met the day before. Nirvana snickered and asked Devonta how he was doing.

He replied "Just fine" as he took her hand and helped her into the car. Nirvana peeped out his clothes, which didn't look as bad as they did when she first saw him.

Devonta and his friend were dressed alike. They had on gray pinstripe pants with a matching white button-down shirt and purple ties. It wasn't what Nirvana was used to, but she had planned on looking past all that so she could enjoy the night. After they parked, they walked to the Fox Theater where the play was being performed. As they walked, Devonta was the perfect gentleman. He held her hand and opened the door for her. Even though Devonta wasn't her type of brotha, she somehow knew that he would be her soul mate.

After the play was over, they went to IHOP for a late breakfast where they cuddled up together in a private booth and got to know each other a bit more. Devonta was somewhat corny, but she tried to laugh at every joke he made.

Once they finished eating, their friends dropped Nirvana back at her apartment, where Devonta asked if he could come up. Nirvana had never let anyone into her apartment, so she asked where he lived and asked if she could join him at his place. Devonta agreed, and then they headed back to his place.

He lived in the city, in a basement-style apartment with bars on all the windows. There was only one way in and one way out. They went into his place. Devonta put on some Brian McKnight, and they slow-danced with each other in silence for about twenty minutes or so. She started to get sleepy, so he offered her a place to lie on his water bed. They both lay in the water bed and started to kiss each other softly for the rest of the night. The next morning, she went home with a huge smile on her face. She didn't know why she was so happy, but she was.

Six months had passed since Nirvana and Devonta had been dating. Nirvana was starting to feel sick but thought she had come down with a bug. Weeks passed by, and she was still feeling sick. She decided to go to the doctor, where she was informed she was pregnant with Devonta's child. She was in so much disbelief that she asked if they could retest her.

"There's no need to retest you. We took your blood, and the level of HCG in your blood tells us you are about three months pregnant," the nurse told her with a smile on her face.

Nirvana was in disbelief. She was not mentally ready for any kids, and she didn't want to have any children out of wedlock.

Chapter 33

The Argument

Although Nirvana wasn't ready to bear a child, she was eager to tell Devonta the news. She called him over to tell him the news. When he came up to her apartment, she greeted him with a huge hug.

"What's this all about?" he asked.

Nirvana took a huge breath and exhaled deeply, saying, "I'm pregnant."

"Whoa, whoa, whoa! You are what? I ain't ready for no kids. What I'mma do with a kid? My girlfriend is going to kill me!" he yelled.

"Wait—you got a girl? You didn't think to tell this the whole six months we been dating?" she screamed at him.

"No, because me and you are only special friends. We were not an item!" he screamed back.

"But you thought it was cool to have unprotected sex with me and nut all up in me? What kind of shit is that, Devonta?"

"You said you were on the pill."

"I was, but does that make you not use your damn common sense to protect not just me but you? So don't blame this on me. Fine—you don't want it. Well, I will just get an abortion. I will call the clinic tomorrow and set up an appointment!" she yelled back. It was not her plan to get rid of a child that was growing in her. She just wanted to see Devonta's reaction.

Devonta looked at her and said, "You will not kill our child. I don't believe in that."

Nirvana felt relieved to hear him say that, but she still had to act tough.

"I should have talked to you about this, but I am not really with my ex–girlfriend. We were on a break. I asked her to marry me, and she turned me away. We still talk, and I was hoping that we would get back together. And I am also getting ready to go in the US Marine Corps," he explained to Nirvana.

Nirvana turned her face away so that he could not see the tear that fell from her eye. All she could think about was being a single parent and having to raise a child all alone. It was something she had already accepted because all she had seen were men walking in and out of the lives of women who had contributed to raising her. She had seen women in her family being dragged by men, and the women screaming and begging on their knees because they were trying to hold on to a man that was walking out on them. Nirvana had made a vow to herself that she would never beg for a man to stay with her. If he wanted to leave, it was something she would just have to get over. She knew and felt that she could do whatever she had to do on her own, and there was no turning back now.

Chapter 34

Preparation

Nirvana was now six months pregnant, and it was time for her to give herself a baby shower. She and Devonta were still communicating with each other, but he still was not over his ex-girlfriend Shelia.

Every time he would come around, he would tell Nirvana that he loved her and wanted to be with her, but it felt like he was stuck between two large rocks and couldn't move. He would also tell her that she was a good woman, and he knew she was the only one for him. It's just that he had given his heart to someone that walked all over it, and he had wanted it to work out between them.

While she planned her baby shower, she asked Devonta for help so that she could get the things she needed for the baby shower. He helped her and also told her he wanted to attend as well. Nirvana was really happy and asked Devonta to invite his parents so that she could finally meet them.

Devonta hesitated by saying, "You don't wanna meet my mother. She is a piece of work. Now my father—he is cool as a fan."

Nirvana didn't ask any more questions but was persistent because she wanted her own family. All she had were her two brothers, and one of them had moved way up to the Northwest, and she had not seen him for many years. Her other brother was around but still had his own life to deal with. The only thing she could imagine was finally having someone accept her as their daughter and her child to enjoy the experience of having grandparents, since her parents were not around anymore to have such a wonderful experience.

Even though Nirvana was not ready to be a mother, it was still one of the happiest moments of her life.

Chapter 35

The Baby Celebration

It was cold and windy outside, and Nirvana was heading over to her aunt Empress's house, where the baby shower was to be held. When she got there, they all worked together to prepare the food and games. Even though Nirvana was about seven months, you couldn't tell because all her weight gain was mostly in her hips and butt. Everyone she invited attended.

Devonta attended the celebration for about ten minutes and then had some of his homeboys pick him up where they all went on dates with a group of girls. As he left the house, Nirvana looked out of the window to see him get into a car full of girls and two of his friends. She felt so disrespected but had to play it cool, because she didn't want anyone at the baby shower to know how she was really feeling.

When she went back into the room where everyone was celebrating her soon-to-be arrival, she sat down next to her aunt Empress, who had tears in her eyes.

"What's wrong with you? Why are you tearing all up?" she asked her aunt.

"Oh, it's just so sad. You look just like your mother. I wish she was here to witness this," she told Nirvana.

Nirvana didn't really buy what her aunt Empress was saying. Even though Nirvana still came around her aunt Empress, she still had suspicions of her having something to do with her mother's death, or at least she knew something about what happened. Now that Nirvana was pregnant, her senses were heightened and her intuition never misled her.

She had also been having tons of dreams and visions surrounding her mother's death, and the vivid scenes were starting to replay in her head.

Nirvana just found it weird that every time she would come around her aunt Empress, Empress would, most of the time, tear up and break out into tears. That was not normal to Nirvana. Her mother had been gone for almost ten years, and all her mom's other sisters did not react the same way.

The baby shower continued to go on. Everyone was enjoying themselves while Nirvana opened all the gifts she was lavished with.

After the baby shower was over with, Nirvana went home, laid down on her couch, and started to wonder why everyone else's wounds had healed from her mother's death except for one person's.

Chapter 36

Delivery

Devonta had finally enlisted into the military and had been sent off to boot camp. He had come by to visit Nirvana before he left. They made love, and he went on his way. He informed her that he would be back in nine weeks when his boot camp was over. To her, that was a long time because she knew he would not be there for the delivery, but she was happy for him.

A few weeks later, Nirvana woke up with horrible pains in her lower abdomen. She called the nurse care line, and they told her to come in to be evaluated. When she arrived, they told her she was having Braxton Hicks contractions. She had only dilated two centimeters, so they sent her home.

Later that evening, the pains came back, but they were more horrendous than the first. The pains were coming every two to three minutes. When she stood up to go get her phone so that she could call the nurse care line again, her water broke, and she fell to the floor. She started to panic and scream because the pains seemed to get worse.

A neighbor noticed a noise coming from her apartment and knocked on the door. "Nirvana, are you all right?" the neighbor asked.

Nirvana yelled, "I think I am in labor."

Her neighbor opened the door to find her on the floor, panting for oxygen and in pain. Her neighbor then called for help. "I need an ambulance! My neighbor is in labor!" They said when they called 911.

Since Nirvana lived downtown, the ambulance was there in ten minutes and transported her to the hospital where she gave birth immediately after she arrived. Nirvana had given birth to a beautiful, healthy boy. She named him after his father. *He's so precious,* she thought to herself when the doctors laid him on her chest. When they laid her new son on her chest, she looked at one of the nurses and whispered, "He has his dad's butt."

The nurse giggled and rubbed Nirvana's head and said, "Awww, how cute."

Chapter 37

Welcome Back

Nirvana had now been a new mommy for two weeks now.

Devonta Jr. was coming along all right. He was cute and healthy, and that was all Nirvana wanted. She just got news that Devonta had graduated boot camp and was coming home later that night for about two weeks. Then he would have to return to finish some other training. She was so excited that he would finally get to see his son.

Later that evening, Devonta was at her door. She was so excited to see him she jumped up on him and gave him a huge hug then pulled his hand so that he could come in to see his son. Devonta held his son and laid him on his chest. To Nirvana, that was the happiest day of her life.

"Did you miss me?" she asked Devonta.

He replied, "Of course, I did."

But Nirvana could tell that his mind was somewhere else.

Devonta had arrived in his full marine uniform and was hot. He decided to take off his uniform so that he could lie on the couch and take a nap. Nirvana put their son in his crib and lay on the couch next to him. Devonta started to rub on her vigorously while trying to take off her clothes.

"What are you doing?" she asked.

"Trying to get some," he replied.

Nirvana stood up instantly and looked down on Devonta. "You know I just had your baby. The doctor said no sex for six weeks. Plus I am still bleeding somewhat. I can't do that to myself."

Devonta sat up and looked at her for about two minutes, and then he started to grab his clothes.

"Where are you going?" she asked.

"Away from here. I haven't had any ass in nearly two months, and you telling me you can't have sex with me. That is bullshit. I am out!" he yelled while putting on his clothes.

"What! Are you serious? You are that self-centered that you don't understand that? What type of person are you?" she screamed.

"The kind that is not going to hang around," he said as he walked out of the door and left Nirvana standing there with tears in her eyes.

The next day Nirvana had tried calling Devonta, but she could not get a hold of him. She had tried his brother and best friend, and they both told her they had not heard from him. She knew they were covering for him, but what was she to expect from his family and best friend? So she waited patiently at her apartment, thinking he would call sometime soon, but he didn't. Before you knew it, a whole week had gone by and still no word from Devonta.

Nirvana kept calling his best friend for answers. For a while, his friend was telling her he didn't know where Devonta was at. Nirvana made one more attempt to call his friend because she knew he had known something. She waited patiently then decided to call his friend back. When his friend answered the phone, she yelled, "I know you know where he is at. He has a son over here, and he has only seen him for a few hours!"

"OK, I will tell you, but don't put my name in it. He is with Shelia. I normally wouldn't even do this, but I am so sick and tired of you calling me. You know, Shelia went to his graduation with his parents. She also drove back with them as well."

Nirvana was so hurt because she felt like she and his son should have been there to support him, but no one shared that information with her. She sat on the couch with tears in her eyes. She told herself enough was enough and she was not going to take any of the disrespect anymore.

The last day of Devonta's visit had finally approached. Nirvana was sitting on the couch when her phone rang. She answered the phone eagerly to find that it was Devonta. He asked her if he could come see her and his son before he left. She agreed.

When Devonta came up to see his son, Nirvana immediately snapped. "What the hell is your problem? Just because I can't have sex at this time, you just gone walk out on your son and stay away for nearly two weeks with that bitch Shelia? If she was a real woman, she would have at least told you to get to know your son, but she is just like your damn folks. Now it is time for you to go back!" she screamed at Devonta. "You haven't even given me any money for him, and I know you got it."

"How much do you want?" Devonta said with a smile on his face as he reached in his back pocket to pull out his wallet.

"I want everything that's in it!" Nirvana yelled.

Devonta shook his head and counted out $480 while laughing, saying, "Take it. It's not like I can't get more. I am good."

Nirvana snatched the money and put him out of her apartment.

Chapter 38

Intimihaters

Nirvana had just gotten up to start her day when her phone rang. She looked at the caller ID but didn't recognize the phone number. "Hello?" she said when she heard the other voice on the other end say "Is this Nirvana?"

"Yes, who am I speaking with?" she asked.

"This is Shelia."

Nirvana's mouth dropped because she didn't even know how Shelia had gotten her phone number. "OK. Well, what's up?" Nirvana asked.

"Well, for one, I was just coming to you as a woman. I know you have a baby by Devonta and all, but I just wanted to let you know, I am the one he wants to marry. You are no one to him but a piece of ass that just got knocked up because you were young, dumb, and stupid. He doesn't want you. You can't make no pole-dancing bitch into a housewife. So I am telling you that you need to step on."

"See, I am established already. You are not. He can't do anything with you. You are disqualified, Honey Boo Boo."

Nirvana held the phone in disbelief at what she was hearing. *Who talks like that? What in the world is Honey Boo Boo?* she thought as she continued to hold the phone partially away from her ear while looking at the phone at the same time as if it was Shelia. Nirvana then slammed down the phone. Shelia had really upset her.

Moments later, her phone rang again. "Hello," she answered in mellow tone of voice.

This time there was a different voice on the other end. It was Devonta's mother. Before Nirvana could get anything out, his mother started to give to her as well. "Hi, this is Cherie, Devonta's mother."

"Oh, hi. How are you?" Nirvana asked. She had never met his mother before, nor had she ever spoken to her on the phone. She thought this was going to be a good phone call, but it turned ugly right away.

"I am OK. I know I never met you, but I did hear that you were some type of dancer. Is that right?"

"Well, I used to dance. I don't anymore," Nirvana answered.

"Well, good. Because that is the devil in you, and it's not God," Cherie started to say.

Cherie was a religious hypocrite. She always would preach about God and how good he was but was always out to put down someone who didn't stand up to her standards. She didn't even have to meet them for her to pass judgment on them. Cherie continued to say to Nirvana, "I also hear you got this baby by my son. Well, I am gone tell you this. I ain't claiming nothing until I get a DNA test. How do I know that baby ain't one of those men you were dancing for? That's right, I said it.

"Besides, Devonta has a beautiful woman already right over here. They are getting married. He already has her engagement ring." She had really given it to Nirvana.

Nirvana was not the type to argue with anyone. She also never had the opportunity to speak her mind, because she was always kept secluded from others when she was young, so she never would argue with anyone because she didn't know what to say or how to say what she felt like she needed to say.

"Well, Devonta never asked me for one. Until he does, that's when I will get one," Nirvana said in a calm voice.

"He doesn't have to because I am!" Cherie yelled.

Nirvana couldn't take another minute of the harassment and slammed the phone down then took it off the hook. Her stomach had started to turn, and she felt nauseated. She continued to get dressed and headed down to the lobby to catch a cab to her brother's house.

Chapter 39

Shattered Love

Nirvana was in the bed resting when she heard a knock at her door. Before she opened the door, she looked though the peephole to notice it was Devonta. She was somewhat happy and sad at the same time.

She opened the door and stood in front of the doorway so that he couldn't enter. "What is it? Why are you here, Devonta?"

"I just want to talk to you. I really need to talk to you."

"OK, only for a few minutes," she said as she moved out his way to let him in.

"I thought you were in some type of training still? Why are you back?" she asked.

Devonta started to tell her that he's allowed to come home every other weekend.

"OK, whateva. What's up?" Nirvana asked, trying to play hard to hide her true feelings for Devonta.

Devonta paced her floor back and forth, saying, "I don't really know how to tell you this. I know we are not committed to each other, but I have decided to be with Shelia. I have to leave you alone altogether."

"Isn't that what you have done already, nigga? Those hoes already called my phone harassing me," she yelled.

"Who and what *H*s are you talking about?" Devonta never liked to use words demeaning to a woman, so he would always say it in a way not to make it sound as bad.

"Your mother and Shelia. They both called me, talking crazy and upsetting me. Your mom asked for a DNA test because she said that is the only way she would say that Li'l D is her grandchild, because he looked more like me! And Shelia was right along with her! Did you put her up to ask me for one? Is that what you want? Because I will give you one with no problem!" she continued to scream.

Devonta sat down on the couch with his hand on his forehead like what he had heard was a lot to take in. "OK, no, I do not want a test. I know our son is mine. I just can't believe my mother would do something like that."

"Well, believe, because she did it."

Devonta stood up so that he could leave. Before he left, he told Nirvana that the marines was sending him to Virginia to go on a six-month tour with the USS *Constellation* and that he would not be able to call unless they were in port somewhere, but he could still get e-mails.

"So when is this supposed to happen?" Nirvana asked.

"Ummm, like in the next few weeks. When I get there, we will still be in port for a while before we leave. You can call this number to ask for me, and they will get me," he told her before leaving out of the door.

Chapter 40

Vulnerable by Fault

"Hey, girl, what you up to? We should get out today!" Twyla said to Nirvana on the other end of the phone.

"Yeah, I should, since I don't have the baby today, right? Plus I am single again! I guess I need to find me a new good man," Nirvana said as she was wiping her eyes because she had just woken up.

"Well, be ready at one 'cause I ain't trying to be out all night 'cause I got a hot date," Twyla told her.

After they hung up the phone, Nirvana got up and found the cutest outfit in her closet to put on. It had been such a long time since she had been out, and it didn't look like she had even had a baby. It was now one o'clock, and Nirvana could see Twyla pull up in front her apartment, so she headed down.

First, they went to the mall to go grab some shoes by Bobbie Jae' and a few shirts by Calvin Klein. Later, they had lunch at an upscale café.

"How many is in your party?" the waiter asked before he seated them.

"Girl, you see how fine this brotha is?" Nirvana mumbled as she elbowed Twyla in the side.

Before they sat down, Twyla looked at the waiter and said to him, "OK, what's your name? We need to know who gone be serving us and tossing our salads?"

"De'Nicko," he said, smiling and shaking his head while walking away.

De'Nicko was a brother from another type of mother. His frame was chiseled to perfection. He was definitely in shape. His height stood at a mere inch over six feet. His skin glowed like the reflection of the sunlight.

"Girl, he just right for some stress sex," Twyla joked.

But Nirvana was sure in agreement with her. They both decided to have endless salads and soups. When De'Nicko brought the bowl of salad out, he asked if they would like any crushed pepper and shredded cheese on their salads. Nirvana and Twyla both looked at each other, deviously smiling, almost saying in harmony, "Yes! Yes! We do! Can you toss them too? It would be so appreciated." Twyla continued to add.

De'Nicko knew they were obviously having fun with him, and he appreciated the laugh while he was working. De'Nicko remained professional and started to grind the pepper over their salads while discreetly moving his hips in harmony with the grinding of the pepper. This move was only noticed by Nirvana and Twyla. They both smiled at each other while they enjoyed every bit of it.

After he finished teasing them, he asked them if their orders were to be on the separate or the same checks.

"Separate!" Twyla hurried and answered.

When De'Nicko returned with their checks, Nirvana was wowed to find that he left his number on the receipt and her bill had a zero balance.

After Twyla took Nirvana home, Nirvana called De'Nikko. De'Nicko asked her if she wanted to step back out because he was trying to get into something.

Nirvana had nothing to do, so she decided to have De'Nikko pick her up, and they ended up going barhopping. Nirvana was having a good time. At about 2:00 a.m., she was ready to go back to her home because she had to get Li'l D early in the morning. De'Nikko took her home. She invited De'Nikko in, and he stayed for a while.

Chapter 41

Mailed Proposal

It had been nearly three months, and Nirvana had not heard anything from Devonta. She had wanted to get out, so she called one of her aunts to ask if she would be willing to babysit so she could have some time to herself. Her aunt agreed to watch Li'l D for a few hours. Nirvana gave Li'l D a bath, put his clothes on, and headed to the lobby to catch a bus. Before catching the bus, she stopped to check her mail. There were five letter-size envelopes in the mailbox from Devonta. Four of the envelopes were really thick, and the other envelope was thin, like it only had a few pages in it. Nirvana sat down in the lobby and opened the thin envelope first. It was a heartfelt letter from Devonta, and it read:

> Hey, how are you doing? I hope fine. I'm up to nothing, just floating on this water. It is really a nice feeling to see something different for once. Anyhow, I am writing to tell you that I am sorry for everything that I have done. Cheating on you and taking you for granted. I am really sorry. I prayed to God and asked him to show me the way. He showed me that you were the one for me and that is why I want you to be my wife.

Nirvana was shocked and couldn't believe what she was reading. She continued to read the rest of the letter.

> I want you to start planning the wedding now. I will be home again the last three weeks of December until the 28th. Whatever you need, I will provide. PS. I love you.

Nirvana sat in the lobby of her apartment with tears in her eyes. She was so excited but didn't know what to do next. She took Li'l D and went back up to her apartment to call her aunt to tell her the news.

She sat on the couch to open the other envelopes that were extremely thick. She opened one envelope slowly to find $3,000 in twenty-dollar bills. She was so surprised she dropped the money on the floor. She thought to herself, *Why would he send cash through the regular mail?* A sheet of paper that was wrapped around the bills read, "Take this money and start planning our wedding." She opened the other envelopes to find $2,000 more in each one. Her eyes were huge.

She had never seen that much money in her life at the same time before. She picked up the phone and called her aunt screaming, "I am getting married! Devonta just proposed and sent me all the money to pay for it."

Her aunt was happy for her and told her to come over the next day so that they could set a date and get things going. Nirvana was so happy. She decided to stay home and relax on her couch and watch television instead.

Chapter 42

Wedding Plans

Nirvana was still thinking about all the money Devonta had sent her.

She was thinking that instead of having a traditional wedding, she and Devonta should go to Jamaica and get married there. It would be less expensive, and it would be a wedding and honeymoon all in one. But she knew Devonta would want an old-fashioned wedding. He and his family were religious freaks and believed everything should be done according to the Bible.

She thought about it but kept the plans. Nirvana chose to have her childhood pastor to join her and Devonta in holy matrimony. Her childhood church was small and old, so her pastor suggested that Nirvana get married in his childhood church. Nirvana went to go check out the church he suggested and instantly fell in love with it. It was one of the largest churches she had ever been in. The church had tall cathedral ceilings with detailed drawings of Jesus and the angels. It was beautiful to Nirvana.

Later that evening, Nirvana and one of her aunts went to a print shop to get invitations printed to send out to family and friends. Everything was happening so fast. She had to notify family and friends to give everyone sufficient time to make arrangements to attend. The very next day, she went with her aunt and her four bridesmaids to pick out dresses. Her colors were pure white and navy blue. They all then went to go shoe-shopping. *Everything is going according to plan,* she thought.

Chapter 43

The Invitation

Nirvana was taking a break downstairs in the lobby of her apartment when the mailman Marley switched his hips past her while holding his mailbag like a purse and walked in and said, "Hey, cutie! You must got some good booty 'cause you just keep getting some major letters in the mail lately. And from across the country too! Yeah, you got some overseas typa pussy," he joked.

Normally Nirvana would have felt insulted if someone had said something like that to her, but she had known Marley the mailman for most of her life. They were super cool. So she just snatched the mail and laughed while saying, "Cutie do must got some good booty, I guess!"

Nirvana eagerly opened the letter to read what it said, and it was a simple letter saying, "Send an invitation to these addresses for me." The addresses were of his parents, brother, sister, and best friend. Nirvana sent the invitations off immediately.

A few days later, Nirvana was sitting in her kitchen making Li'l D something to eat, and her phone rang. "Hello," she said.

"Ummm, yes, Nirvana, this is Cherie, and I have my sisters Tina and Tammy on the line. See we just received your invitation. What's this all about a wedding? Devonta didn't run this by us. We are his family, and we come first." The voice of Devonta's mother was very sweet when she said it, but you could feel the testiness in her voice.

Then Cherie's sisters started to yell. "So you a stripper? My nephew is marrying a stripper? He is supposed to be with Shelia. She was here first!"

For some reason, Shelia had been around Devonta's family for many years. She was a friend of the family. Shelia and Devonta's sister Ahlonda were like two peas in a pod. They all were determined to become family one way or another. They had a special type of bond.

Nirvana never knew why Devonta's mother had it out for her and passed judgment on her without even getting to know her. His mother was also painting a horrible residual image of Nirvana in other people's minds before they had ever met her. Nirvana took a deep breath and told them in a calm voice, "I have nothing to do with the fact that he wants to marry me! I am who Devonta chose. Obviously, he knows who I really am."

Nirvana was at her boiling point with all the insulting calls. Infuriated, she continued to tell them as well, "Maybe if that bitch hadn't given him Chlamydia before he went to boot camp, she would be with him. Yeah, he called and told me. And guess what? I wasn't even with him at that time. Maybe he would have chosen her if she had said yes the first time he asked her to marry him! Ask her why she was afraid of commitment, but now that I am in the picture, she wants to marry him? Tell that bitch she done missed the last bus. That's your real hoe right there. Yeah, I might dance to get my dollars, honey, but I am not a slut. If you don't know me, don't judge me!"

Nirvana then hung up the phone on them.

Chapter 44

Probed

Nirvana had awakened nauseated the next morning. She was feeling really weak and went to the bathroom and started to vomit uncontrollably into the toilet. She knew something was not right, so she cleaned herself up and quickly went to the urgent care clinic. While waiting for the nurse to take her to the triage room and get her vitals, she started to vomit again. The nurses then hurried to take her vitals and run tests. They had asked her when was the last time she had been sexually active, and she responded, "Some weeks ago to a month or so. I don't know, could have been longer."

The nurse informed her that she was pregnant. Nirvana looked as if someone had just poured a whole bowl of raw eggs over face. She feared because she knew she was not pregnant by Devonta. The last person she had been with was De'Nikko, and they rarely spoke much anymore. Their encounter was temporary, and they had no need to speak anymore. Nirvana hurried and got her things and rushed out of the urgent care in disappointment.

Next, she went home, called Twyla, and cried, telling her the bad news. It was a matter of time before she and Devonta were to unite as one. "I have to tell him," she said to Twyla.

"No! The hell you don't! You better marry his ass and tell him after you have it. I wouldn't tell him nothing if he don't say anything to me. That's how the women in my family roll. Shit, what they don't know won't hurt 'em. Shit, I don't even know if my daddy mines," she joked and laughed.

Nirvana giggled but still knew she had to do the right thing. She didn't want to go into a marriage dishonestly. Trust was everything to her.

Chapter 45

Honesty First

The next day, Devonta called Nirvana to check in on her. She knew this was the time to break the news to him. She didn't want to do it over the phone, but the sooner she got the heavy weight of dishonesty off her shoulders, the faster she would feel better. She also knew that he could say he didn't want to be with her anymore as well. It was a win-lose situation. "I'm pregnant!" she said quickly and abruptly to Devonta.

"You what?" he said in a very vague, shocked voice.

"Yes, I am, and it is not yours. I am so sorry. I just found out a few days ago, and I was shocked too. I know you might not want to marry me now, but I had to tell you the truth," she exclaimed.

Devonta held the phone in silence for about two minutes. You could hear him breathing. He was panting in very calm and controlled breaths. "I am upset to hear that. I am," he began to say.

He continued by saying, "I did break it off with you. I guess I can't expect for you to pause your life because you feel like there might have been an opportunity with us. Life goes on, but I still want to marry you. And that is still my child you are carrying."

Nirvana smiled and cried on the other end of the phone and looked up to the ceiling and said, "Thank you, God!"

They continued their conversation as if what they had just discussed was never spoken about.

Chapter 46

Everything Seems Perfect

It was now a few days before the wedding, and all the last-minute things had to be done. Nirvana and Devonta had just finished the last class of their premarital counseling and were now ready to jump the broom. They didn't really have a honeymoon planned because no one wanted to watch Li'l D and Nirvana was very protective of her only son. So they decided to get a penthouse suite downtown at the Marriott Hotel. The cake and flowers had already been ordered, and it was just a wonderful thing to see everything going according to plan.

Chapter 47

The Night Before

Devonta and Nirvana were lying in the bed, and about 3:00 a.m., Devonta's phone rang. He answered the phone, and you could hear on the other end that it was a woman. It sounded like something was wrong.

When he got off of the phone, he told Nirvana that he had to go because his mother was crying.

Nirvana looked at him and said in a voice of disbelief, "Really, Devonta? The day of our ceremony? Come on now. Do I look like Boo Boo the Fool?"

He didn't respond but reached over and gave her a kiss on the forehead. He left Nirvana in the bed and didn't return until about 7:45 a.m. the next morning.

Chapter 48

Not Reality

The wedding had started, and guests were still arriving. The church was so huge. It had a capacity for about eight hundred or more people.

Nirvana had invited all her family on both her father's and mother's sides of the family. The only guest that had showed up in Devonta's party was his sister Ahlonda, his brother Zeal, and his best friends Larry and Dean. Zeal and Larry were good friends with Nirvana.

Ahlonda couldn't stand Nirvana—she was just there to start some commotion. She had no good motives. Cherie, Devonta's mother, had called him early and told him she wasn't going to be able to make it because she had something more important to do and she didn't approve of his choice.

The wedding went on as planned. Nirvana was escorted down the aisle by her oldest brother, Vadyme, and her uncle Ducc, who was her father's oldest brother. There were four bridesmaids lined up near the altar, all dressed in navy-blue satin gowns and holding coordinating flowers to match. The best men all had on pure white tuxedos with navy blue ties and shoes with matching corsages pinned on their tuxedos.

As Nirvana was escorted down the aisle, she heard a low, faint voice singing "You are flesh of my flesh." As she got closer, Devonta's voice grew stronger. Tears began to roll down her face. When she reached Devonta, he held her hand and continued to vocalize with his strong voice.

After Devonta sang, the ring bearer, Vadyme's son, dressed in a navy-blue suit and white tie, brought the rings. Nirvana's ring was a gold wedding band encrusted with small diamonds along the band while Devonta's ring was a pure solid gold band.

It was now time to say their vows. Before Pastor Troy had them say their vows, he asked anyone who wanted to say anything to speak up now or forever hold their peace. Ahlonda was sitting on the right side of the church from where Devonta and Nirvana were preparing to say their vows. She slowly raised her hand, but only high enough so that the pastor could not see. She was not brave enough to get up and speak.

"Repeat after me," Pastor Troy instructed Nirvana. Nirvana was still choked up in tears from Devonta's singing to her that when she said her vows, it sounded like gibberish and laughing at the same time. It was so uncontrollable. Next, Devonta said his vows. "You may now kiss your bride," Pastor Troy told him. Devonta took her face and held it like it was the last thing on earth he wanted to do, and he softly kissed her lips.

Chapter 49

The Wedding Channel

The reception was being held on the lower level of the church. Her aunts all helped make the appetizers and dinner to be served. Her cake was a seven-tier cake with a waterfall and topped with strawberries and shavings of white and dark chocolate. While everyone was mingling in the congregation of the church and preparing to head down to the lower level, Devonta told Nirvana that Ahlonda wanted to talk to her. Nirvana felt uneasy about speaking with Ahlonda because she knew the conversation couldn't possibly be a good one. Nirvana agreed to speak with Ahlonda privately. Nirvana and Ahlonda waited until they were the only two left alone in the congregation. Nirvana sat on one of the pews because she was starting to feel nauseated and weak. Nirvana was very intuitive. Her intuition was telling her to prepare for the worst.

Ahlonda stood up in front of Nirvana and said "Congratulations" while turning her mouth to one side looking at Nirvana as if she could slap her. Ahlonda's voice was very raspy and harsh.

"Well, why are you saying it like that? You don't seem happy? I don't even know if I should say thank you, because that was sure not genuine," Nirvana told her.

Ahlonda then began to yell at her, "I am not happy for you. You know who was there first. I swear if you ever hurt my brother I am going to mop the floor with your face."

All of a sudden, another voice came from outside the congregation, behind the door, intruding and saying, "And if anyone ever does anything to my niece, they are going to have to deal with me." It was

Nirvana's uncle Ducc. He had been eavesdropping on the conversation between the two from the beginning. Ahlonda was so shocked and didn't know what to do. She continued to hold her ground. Ducc went down to the lower level, and several minutes later, about ten to twelve people had rushed upstairs in defense of Nirvana.

Nirvana's friend Kikka was there and was the first one that landed on the top flight of stairs leading down to the lower level where Nirvana and Ahlonda were now standing. "Bitch, why you trying to upset my girl on her wedding day and shit?" Kikka said, stepping up to Ahlonda. Everyone else was surrounding Ahlonda.

Ahlonda had no fear in her heart. She stood there quietly and patiently taking off all her jewelry and was ready for anyone who was going to try to attack her first. Nirvana couldn't believe what was happening. Her heart felt like it had dropped from her chest.

Vicki was one of the bridesmaids and was the first one that tried to swing at Ahlonda. "Bitch, I will fuck you up!" Vicki said as she tried to tear Ahlonda's face off.

Ahlonda avoided the punch by moving to the side. While others intervened to keep the commotion down, Devonta then appeared at the top of the stairs with a look of confusion because he had just found out what was going on.

"Your sista trying to start something with your wife. You betta get her 'fore she get her ass whipped!" someone yelled from the crowd.

Nirvana couldn't believe that an almost perfect day had gone bad in just a matter of minutes. She ran downstairs to the bathroom with tears in her eyes and started to puke. Her first mind told her to take off her wedding gown and go do some damage. She waited in the bathroom until everything calmed down. She wiped her last few tears from her puffy face and went to the reception, where Devonta was waiting for her.

Everyone could tell she was upset, because her eyes were red from crying. Nirvana tried to smile, but everyone could tell the smile was not real. It was now time for her and Devonta to cut the first piece of cake. They had both tasted cake off the same plate when Nirvana saw Ducc giving her the signal from across the room to smash the cake into Devonta's face. She smiled and smooshed the cake in Devonta's face.

After the wedding, they both took Li'l D and drove to their penthouse suite downtown. Before she left, her aunt Jean pulled her to the side and told her, "During the reception, a girl had called and asked the pastor if he had married you all."

Nirvana was in shock and couldn't believe all this drama. She then knew she had been married into a family of hypocrites. Nirvana was exhausted, and Devonta's mind was obviously somewhere else. Their so-called honeymoon was just like a normal day of being at home. They didn't have too much to say to each other, and they both just ended up going to sleep.

Chapter 50

One Month Later . . .
On the Bay in Coronado

Nirvana had just moved to California, on the bay where Devonta had been stationed. It seemed like everything was going perfect. Nirvana was enjoying herself. The beach and the water's view she had from her apartment was just breathtaking. Devonta was never there because he was always out working. She was loving the life.

While Devonta was gone, she began to clean the house because she knew he would be coming home soon. As she was washing their laundry, she noticed some papers and what looked like to be receipts in one of Devonta's jackets. She pulled them from the inside pocket of the jacket that they were in.

She didn't plan to look at them, but what caught her attention was a plane ticket receipt that showed Devonta had traveled around Valentine's Day. That bothered her, because he had told her that he was going to be out to sea. She was so hurt. She also saw credit card receipts for gifts and grocery lists. Things weren't, of course, adding up. She had no way of getting in contact with him because he was out working again. She just sat there with her son, Li'l D, and waited to have her next child.

A few weeks later, when Devonta returned home, she asked him to explain the receipts. He told her he went to take his mother flowers in Oklahoma before he left to sea because he had not seen her in almost a year. Nirvana didn't buy what he was saying. She knew it was a lie.

She looked at him and asked. "So you telling me that taking your momma flowers all the way from the other side of the country was more important than us on Valentine's Day? We only been married two months. Really!" Nirvana yelled, "You are a liar! Why did you marry me?"

Devonta never answered her. He walked away stubbornly, like what she said didn't matter.

Nirvana started to feel like she was trapped all over again.

Chapter 51

When Reality Became Reality

Months had gone by, and Devonta still acted as if what Nirvana had asked him did not matter.

He had really started to change. Devonta was sweet and kind at all times, he did not curse, nor did he ever get angry. He was a very spiritual person and knew the Bible like no other, but he had some serious issues. He was very stubborn and all for himself. He and Nirvana had only been married a few months, and everything was starting to fall apart all over Devonta's greed. Their relationship was like water and fire. He was fire, and she was like water. They had no communication, and both wanted to have the last say-so. Nirvana had been imprisoned too long before from speaking her mind, and she was not going to keep letting things go.

Later on, Shelia started to call their house and demand to speak with Devonta. Nirvana would always ask Devonta how Shelia got the number, and he would say from his mother or sister. Nirvana would plead with him to ask them not to disrespect her. He never did. For some reason, he let his mother control his thought process. Cherie continued to cause problems in their marriage. Nirvana was getting fed up. She had no family where she was, and she barely spoke to anyone back home.

The phone calls continued to come through from all different types of numbers. Every time she would answer, it would always be Ahlonda demanding to speak with Devonta, where she would then put Shelia on the phone. Nirvana always knew when Devonta was talking to Shelia. She could tell by the tone of Devonta's voice.

Nirvana was clearly getting fed up. She never understood how a man could not take a stand against his mother if she was clearly in the wrong. Nirvana wasn't dumb by a long shot. She knew Devonta just wanted to have his cake and eat it too. It was clear that he still had some type of feelings for Shelia. For nearly three years, Shelia and Ahlonda continued to call Nirvana and harass her. Devonta continued to lie about his whereabouts while still continuing to find ways to leave town to go be with Shelia.

Nirvana developed hatred toward Shelia. Nirvana had told herself that she never wanted to go back to Saint Louis ever again. Even though she knew Devonta was going to continue to cheat on her, she decided to stay married to him for the flight. He was her ticket to move all over the world.

Chapter 52

Fourth Time Around

Nirvana was now pregnant with her fourth son. She had just moved to Dallas and found them all a new home since Devonta had just got stationed there for four years. Instead of renting, she decided to go buy a house. She always put everything in Devonta's name. He had given her power of attorney, and with that, she could sign his life away. She ended up finding a three-bedroom ranch home with two car garages right in the midst of all the action. She started to decorate to get the home ready for when Devonta arrived. It felt good to be in a new town. She looked at this move as brand-new start with them. Nirvana was now seven months pregnant.

Weeks later, Devonta arrived. Once he arrived, everything seemed to be cool until his cell phone started to ring off the hook at all hours of the night. Nirvana would always ask him who it was, and he would tell her it was his sister. She knew that he was lying. He would always come to bed at wee hours in the morning. By the time he was coming to the bed, Nirvana was normally waking up to start her day. They were on two completely different schedules.

At Devonta's new duty station, he pushed papers. He didn't have to go back out any tours for four years. One day, when he got home from work, he jumped in the shower and left his phone out on the bed. It had started to ring.

Nirvana decided to answer his phone, and whoever was on the other line hung up instantly. Nirvana then called the number back from a different number and a voice of a woman said "Hello." Nirvana proceeded to introduce herself to the lady and ask her who she was and why was she calling her husband.

The lady said to Nirvana in a giggling, childish voice, "Ask him, not me. I ain't calling him. He call me, and I am returning the call."

Nirvana politely asked the lady to not call anymore and hung up the phone. When Devonta got out of the shower, she asked him, "Who is this?" holding his phone in his face so that he could see the phone number.

"I don't know. Who they say they were?"

"You know who the hell this is. I am tired of all these women calling you and you acting like my feelings don't matter. Why do you keep getting me pregnant if you don't want to be with me? And for most, why in the hell did you ask me to marry you?" she screamed at him while holding her baby bump as if she was in pain.

Devonta then started to tell her, "OK, her name is Rosetta. She works with me. She is a contracted employee that was assigned here for a few months. Nothing is going on. She just asked me if I could work out with her so that she could lose some weight."

"Bull crap, nigga. What kind of weight? I am up here getting ready to have your fourth son, and you are talking about helping some woman lose weight?" She asked while rolling her neck and eyes at Devonta. She continued to tell him to tell the lady no and that she was not comfortable with them exercising together.

Devonta agreed to it and said he would end the relationship, since it was nothing to begin with in the first place. Nirvana believed him, even though she felt she was still being lied to.

Chapter 53

Push

"Push! Push! Push! Push! Push!" the nurse yelled.

Nirvana pushed as hard as she could. The room started to go dark to Nirvana. Her lips were turning blue, and the baby was breeched. Nirvana had to have an emergency C-section. Devonta was instructed to leave and go in the waiting room for a while. Forty-five minutes later, the surgeon came out to tell Devonta he was the father of a healthy baby boy and that Nirvana was doing OK and that he would be able to see them shortly. Devonta was relieved to know that everything was OK. For a split second, he did fear of possibly losing Nirvana.

Chapter 54

Early A.M.

Nirvana and their new son had been released from the hospital. It had been about two days that she had been home. On the third day, Nirvana was awakened by Devonta getting ready to leave out of their bedroom at about 5:00 a.m. She quickly got up and asked, "Where are you going?"

"Oh, I am just getting ready to work out over here at the Air Force base. I will be back at 7:30," he said to her.

Nirvana nodded and laid back down. She didn't ask him any more questions. When he came back, he was drenched as if water had been poured on him in a pattern on his shirt to make it seem as if he had been working out. "I hope you had a nice workout," she said to him as he came into the room and went straight to the shower. Nirvana was tired and had a feeling of disbelief, but she didn't bother to elaborate on it. When Nirvana lived in California, she had a friend named Porsh that was dealing with a married man named Reece. Porsh and Nirvana were really close and had developed an unbreakable friendship. Porsh had told Nirvana one day that she asked Reece what he told his wife when he would be gone for long hours. Reece had told Porsh that he would tell his wife that he was at the gym and that he would pour water on himself so that he would appear to be sweating. While thoughts were replaying in her head, she tried not to think about it. They had just had another son, and she wanted everything to be all right.

Chapter 55

Baby, These Are My Confessions

It was just a few weeks before Christmas and a week before Devonta and Nirvana's sixth anniversary. She was driving home from the local grocery store when she saw Devonta going somewhere when he was supposed to be at work. He was getting on the freeway, heading southbound and talking with a huge smile on his face to someone on the phone. She called him on his cell phone and asked him what he was doing.

"Oh, nothing. Taking a friend home from work. They didn't have a ride, so I am dropping them off," he told her.

Now that was a huge lie because she had just seen him, and no one was in his car. She decided to go on home and wait patiently for him. When he came home, as soon as he walked in the door, she asked him, "What the hell is going on?" She demanded answers from him immediately.

She sent the children upstairs to their rooms. Nirvana and Devonta sat on the chestnut brown leather sectional that was in their living room. She looked at him with the rage of a madwoman while he started to confess his problems.

"Baby, I do love you, but I have problems," he began to say. "Every time I told you I had to go out of town, most of the time, I was with Shelia."

Nirvana was not too much worried about Shelia anymore, because it had been nearly two years since she had any issues with Shelia. She knew they still talked, but just didn't even care anymore. Nirvana looked at him and said, "I forgive you as long as she was the last person you were with. Because that was about two years ago."

Devonta held his head down and said, "No, there's more." He went on to tell her that two weeks before she had their last son, he had been with one of the girls she had contacted in the past.

Nirvana had seen text messages from the possible girl he was telling her about but just tried to overlook everything that was wrong in her relationship. It was hard for Nirvana to understand that she did not have to accept that type of abuse from anyone. She didn't have any real women in her life to tell her otherwise. She thought that was the way of life.

Devonta continued to ramble on about how he worked out with Rosetta even though she didn't approve. He was telling it all. "I have problems. I love women and sex. I don't know what's wrong with me."

Nirvana didn't care about what he had just said. What had got her attention was when he said he had been working out with Rosetta. "And when was this?" she asked. He began to tell her it started a few days after she had come home with their last child. "What!" she yelled. Nirvana was devastated because when she was sent home from the hospital, she still had staples in her stomach from the C-section she had with their last son. During that time, she was instructed by the doctor not to go up and down the stairs unless she really had to, and if she did, to sit and go up and down the steps and do the same for coming back up the stairs. Devonta knew this. "So you thought being at home with your wife, who had staples in her stomach, and your son was much less important than working out with someone because they need to lose some weight? That it some bullshit!" she yelled at him. Nirvana was now at her boiling point with Devonta.

Chapter 56

Confrontation

Nirvana felt like she had to confront Shelia just to let her know that she had known she was still dealing with Devonta long after they had got married. When she called her house, the voice of a man answered the phone, and Nirvana asked for Shelia.

The voice told her that she wasn't in, but proceeded to ask, "Um, is this Nirvana?"

"Yes," she replied.

"Hey, my name is Orah. I am now Shelia's boyfriend, but what I wanted to know is, do you live in Dallas?"

"Yes," she answered.

He continued talk, "I am just so glad that I was able to speak with you, because Shelia told me she was coming down there. It didn't make any sense to me. She claimed to be coming with Devonta's mother. I knew that was bullshit." He kept on talking, telling Nirvana that Devonta's mother was planning a surprise reunion for him and Shelia that he had heard them talk about on the phone one day, but he didn't say anything to her about it.

Nirvana was shocked but believed every bit of what she was hearing. She already knew not to ask Devonta because she knew he would say he had no knowledge of anything. After Nirvana had finished speaking with Orah, she hung up the phone. Moments later, her phone was ringing back, and it was Shelia and Ahlonda, both on the phone and calling to jump down her throat. When she answered the phone, Shelia immediately screamed, "Bitch, why you calling my phone?"

Ahlonda immediately said right afterward, "Bitch, we gone whip your ass when we see you!"

Nirvana went on to tell Shelia that she didn't have time to argue and all she wanted was to let her know that she knew, and whatever she did would come back to her double.

Shelia giggled on the phone, saying, "Yeah, whatever. You just mad 'cause he was still in love with me. Get over it. He never wanted you. He just married you because you had his first child."

Nirvana shook her head and hung up the phone.

Chapter 57

Karma Jolt

It had been months since the confrontation with Shelia, and all the drama seemed like it was calming down. Nirvana had started to read a book called *Teach Me How to Love You* so that she could work on her marriage with Devonta.

Devonta had just gotten off the phone with his sister. He was happy that he was about to be an uncle. Ahlonda already had had one son by one of Shelia's cousins. She and Shelia did anything possible to say that they were related. This time, the baby was supposed to be by an older guy she was dealing with across the state somewhere.

Months went on when Devonta got a call from his brother Zeal telling him that Ahlonda was really pregnant by Orah, the daddy of Shelia's twin boys. All the while that Ahlonda was on Shelia's side when it came to Nirvana, she was screwing her best friend all along.

Shelia had twin boys by Orah a few years after Devonta married Nirvana. It was sad to see this happening between them, but Nirvana felt relieved. She went into the kitchen of their home and made some margaritas. Devonta didn't drink, so she indulged in the whole pitcher. After getting drunk, she started to say to Devonta, "You know, I am happy it happened this way. Your sister had given Shelia all the blankets and pillows in the world to make her feel comfortable. When you think about it, I guess it is cool that folks do think about your best interest when they are fucking you, but it's even more fucked up when when you comfortable and you don't even know you being fucked. I think God works things in mysterious ways. Your slut sister is preggo by her best friend's man. That is so sickening. They really wanted to be related. Well, they will be now for sure 'cause Ahlonda's first kid is now Sheila's kid's cousin. And the child she is carrying is also her cousin and sister. One big happy family!"

Nirvana raved around the house. "I knew this shit was gone come to an end soon," she continued to say. Before she finished talking, she told Devonta that she thought God made that happen between them for a reason, because if it had not happened, he would still be continuing to see Shelia. She made jokes telling him that if he ever had sex with Shelia again, it would be like having sex with his own sister, since Ahlonda had taken her leftovers and continued to blindly share Orah with Sheila.

Devonta looked disgusted by the thought of it. The next day, while Devonta was at work, Nirvana packed her bags along with her kids and put them in the brand-new car they had just purchased and headed to Saint Louis to go be with her brother Vadyme.

Chapter 58

I Hope You Read My Letter

Before leaving, Nirvana sat at the kitchen table, thinking about everything she had gone through with Devonta and his family. She poured herself a cup of coffee and lit a cigarette while writing him a letter from the heart. Nirvana always had expressed her feelings better on paper. Every time she tried to tell Devonta how she felt, she would end up crying and wouldn't be able to get her words out completely.

The letter read

> Hey, I hope you read this letter. I just need you to fathom me. When I first met you, you seemed like the perfect type of guy. We went out on a date, and we didn't stay out too late. It seemed like we became the best of friends. I don't care about the things that happened before our marriage, but I do care about what happened during and after we were married. I always told you everything. I trusted you with my mind, heart, and body, but you continued to misuse them. Before I met you, I had my own life. I made my own money. My self-esteem was high like the sky.
>
> What is love? What is it supposed to feel like? If love is all about someone constantly taking you for granted and walking all over your heart, I don't think I want to ever love again. I remember when you asked me to give up my

pleasures. I did because you were my husband. I asked you, and you said, "Get over it! It's nothing." Well, I think I just got over it.

Good-bye, Devonta.

Nirvana sealed the letter in an envelope scented with Envy the Girl, a fragrance that Devonta loved for her to wear. She left the envelope on his pillow in their bedroom. She took a big breath and smiled as she left all her unhappiness in the house.

Chapter 59

Expired Visit

It had been three weeks since Nirvana had been back home in Saint Louis with her brother Vadyme. Vadyme had just purchased a new home and welcomed her there for as long she needed. Later that day, Vadyme asked Nirvana if she had spoken with Devonta recently. She told him no. Vadyme then told her even if she didn't want to speak with him, she needed to communicate with her husband. It was something that needed to be done. "I love you, sis, but you must go back home. You have to face the music one day," Vadyme explained.

Nirvana took a deep breath and replied, "Yeah, I know. You are right. Honestly, I was planning to leave tonight."

Chapter 60

Incomplete

Devonta and Nirvana's relationship was not the best. There was never any communication between the two of them. It had been about three months since Nirvana had been back home with Devonta. Their relationship wasn't getting any better. Nirvana was still feeling down. Her self-esteem still had not taken flight. Nirvana's mind was idle, which made her vulnerable to the temptations of the world, all because she and Devonta didn't know how to communicate with each other. They both loved each other dearly, but they were too stubborn for each other. Together their force was magnetic. Nirvana was like water, and Devonta was like fire. Together they ignited steam. They were completely opposite of each other, but his fire calmed her water storms, and her storms calmed his fires. Fire and water can destroy the world in seconds. Alone, Nirvana and Devonta were each like venomous serpents looking to devour anything in their paths. Their home was completely broken. While steam can cause painful scars, eventually the steam will cool down and the scars would heal. They were opposites but good for each other.

Nirvana was at the point in her life where she was tired of being misused, lied to, and disappointed. Her marriage was not the best. She wasn't happy and felt that Devonta was still the same person. He never felt that he needed to take a personal inventory of himself. Nirvana had started to realize that the same patterns Devonta had before they were married he still retained them. It was time that she stood up and communicated with her husband.

It was noon when she came to a conclusion of what she was going to say to her husband and how she would say it. Nirvana felt that the patterns Devonta chose to tote around with him were a curse from his family. Devonta's family possessed many demonic strongholds. Even though Devonta was raised up in church and his family worshipped faithfully, they were spiritually demented folks. Nirvana believed that her husband had a sexual spirit upon him. Devonta couldn't go without some form of sexual pleasure for more than a day. When Nirvana was asked to describe Devonta to others, she would always laugh first and say, "He is just like Tiger Woods. He just doesn't play golf." When she would say that, those asking always thought she meant perfect. Devonta always carried himself in such a way that no one would ever think he would harm a fly. He was presentable at all times. When Devonta came home later that day, Nirvana decided not talk to Devonta about what was on her mind, because she knew the conversation would be headed toward a dead end.

Sequel Preview

Nirvana was tired of depending on Devonta's income. She had taken so much from him. He was a good man when it came down to supporting financially. Devonta gave Nirvana anything she wanted. Nirvana was at point in her life where she wanted to be able to maintain on her own. All the good Devonta had done for her, she felt like it was because he felt like he owed her something for all the wrong he had done and all the lies he had told her. Nirvana also knew that he finally was realizing that she was an amazing woman, and with the empire she was currently building, she could sift through his fingers forever. Nirvana had an outgoing entrepreneurial spirit. She always followed her dreams. She had managed to start a nonprofit organization called ENVY. Nirvana became one of the highest-paid self-made entrepreneurs in the Midwest. All her pain was finally digested, and she had achieved her state of true bliss.

The Decree

About the Author

Nirvana Pride, a.k.a. Mrs. NV, is an entrepreneur. She is from and currently resides in Saint Louis, Missouri, with her husband and four children. She went to Pima Medical Institute in Chula Vista, California, to be a certified medical assistant and phlebotomist. Later, she returned to school to become a certified chef at L'Ecole Culinaire in Clayton, Missouri.

Nirvana owns NVme Boutique in Saint Louis, Missouri, and plans to franchise in every state that she has lived in. Nirvana has been in local newspaper publications and has a strong sense of fashion and style. She loves to help others feel *amazing* about themselves and mentors troubled young girls.

This is her first publication, and she is very enthusiastic about it. Nirvana would love to hear from her readers at fathomnirvana@gmail.com.

About NVme Boutique

NVme Boutique started its journey October 1, 2011, with hope in mind that we will be able to captivate our customers with an envied style that only they would be able to rock in their own unique way. We believe fashion is not all about following the current trend, but fashion is what we make it to be. Our motto: "Why eNVy them when they can eNVy you?" It's pretty catchy, huh?

Who wants someone wearing the same thing they are? No one does. That's why most fashion-forward folks shop at boutiques, right? That's what being different and unique is all about. That's why here at NVme Boutique, we dare you to be different. NVme Boutique offers a wide range of high-quality, fashionable, pocket-savvy pieces for ladies and gentlemen, from tops, bottoms, shoes, outerwear, accessories, and handbags.

NVme Boutique believes that we will always be a proven trendspotter. We believe our boutique will always be ahead of the current trends, making our customers a trendsetter in their own world. NVme is an empowerment statement, an attitude, and a fashion statement. If you always feel as if someone envies you, then you have no reason to feel insecure about who you are, what someone thinks about you, how you look or feel. No one knows how you are feeling unless you tell them. NVme was established for all genres of individuality, to empower them to feel *amazing* about themselves despite who they are, where they come from, or how they look or feel.

So say it loud: *NVme!* Visit us online at www.nvmeboutiqueshop.com.

Bobbi Ja'e

Extras

Entrepreneur. A person who organizes a business or businesses by taking financial risks to do so. Also a promoter in the entertainment industry.

Nirvana. The ideal condition of rest, harmony, stability, and joy. It's the ultimate state of liberation from unhappiness. It's the illumination characterized by the merging of an individual, departing from unhappiness and entering into an entirely different mode of existence. To achieve nirvana, you have to overcome three wholesome roots: undisciplined desire, hatred, and delusion. Nirvana, simply put, means satisfaction, happiness, bliss, "taming the fire with water," "blowing out the candle."

Vivacious. Full of high spirits, animation, lively or vital, bubbling, sparkling, spirited.

Youthful. Young in spirit and heart.

Index

A

Ahlonda (Devonta's sister), 106, 112-15, 119-20, 127-30

B

Bobbie (mother), 13-16, 18-19, 22, 24, 26-27

C

Cherie (Devonta's mother), 97, 105, 112, 119
Chicago, 66, 68, 70-71
Choclik, 61, 63, 69, 73
Club Contagious, 53, 58-60, 65-67, 69, 81
Collins, Maxine (aunt), 13-15, 19-23
Crystal, 30, 35, 38

D

De'Nikko, 101, 107
Devonta, 81, 83-85, 87, 89, 91, 93-99, 102-7, 109-27, 129-35, 137
Devonta Jr., 93
Ducc (uncle), 38-40, 112, 115

E

Earl, 70
Ein, 66, 69, 72, 78
Empress (aunt), 13-18, 20-22, 28, 89-90

F

Fayetteville, North Carolina, 13, 19, 24

G

Gayeilla, 70, 78
Georgjae, 76

H

Havana Nights, 65, 81

I

Independence Day, 24, 31

J

Jae (Georgjae), 72, 76-78, 80
Jean (aunt), 30, 35, 115

K

Kat (grandmother), 23, 26-27, 29-30, 33, 36-40
Kelly (step-aunt), 29-30, 64
Kikka (classmate), 42-47, 49, 115

L

Labor Day, 15, 17, 31
Lil Bitty Bit (cousin), 37
Li'l D, 99, 101-3, 105, 110, 115, 117

M

Magnificent Mile, Chicago, 71, 76-77
Mason (grandfather), 27, 29, 39
Mauhget (aunt), 30-31, 33-35, 38
Maxine Collins, 13

N

Nirvana, 13-20, 22-81, 83-135, 137, 142, 146

O

Orah, 127, 129-30

P

Parice (aunt), 56-57

R

Rick, 16
Ronzell, 46-47
Rosetta, 122, 126
Rosie, 26-27

S

Saint Louis, Missouri, 13, 23, 31, 120, 130, 133, 142
Sam, 17, 70
Shelia, 87, 94-96, 98-99, 106, 119-20, 125, 127-30
Shot Gun, 25

T

Ted, 54-55, 58-61, 63, 66-68, 80-81
Twyla, 52-55, 58, 61-63, 68, 81-83, 100-101, 107

V

Vadyme (brother), 35-36, 39-40, 58, 112, 130, 133
Vicki (cousin), 30-31, 35, 115

Y

Yummi (best friend), 62-63, 66-67, 69-76, 78-79, 81

Z

Zeal (Devonta's brother), 112, 129

FATHOM ME

SPECIAL EDITION

THIS BOOK WAS GIVEN TO

GIVEN BY

DATE

OCCASION